MW01226600

to Gilb

Daniel W. Hall

A MAN NAMED JOHN

By

Daniel W. Hall

PublishAmerica
Baltimore

First printing

All characters in this book are fictitious, and any resemblance to real persons, living or dead, is coincidental.

PublishAmerica has allowed this work to remain exactly as the author intended, verbatim, without editorial input.

Hardcover 978-1-4560-4066-6
Softcover 978-1-4560-4067-3
PUBLISHED BY PUBLISHAMERICA, LLLP
www.publishamerica.com
Baltimore

Printed in the United States of America

To my Wife
For all her love and patient endurance

Other books by
Daniel W. Hall

Frontier Hearts: The story of Captain John Mathias

From Buckskins to Boots – an illustrated book of poems

Spark of Madness

www.dwhalladventures.com

A MAN
NAMED JOHN

1

It's a hard thing to say what makes a man the way he is. Some say he's just born a certain way, others say God makes him that way and still others say that its life that makes a man what he is. Maybe it's a little bit of all these things. But the real question is; what is it that changes a man?

This is the story of a man named John. I was just a boy of twelve when I first met him, but I think that I shall never forget him. And even though I only knew him for a very short time, no man, other than my own father, has ever made such an impact on my life. He was a big man, and I have never seen a human being as strong, as tough, and as hard as this man that walked past me and Dad the day we were trying to get our wagon unstuck from the mud on the side of the road. It was just Dad and I, Mom had passed away three years before and things had never been the same. We got along as best we could, as good as anyone can that loses the dearest thing to your heart. Dad never complained about much at all, but every now and then I would catch him looking far off at nothing. Sometimes he would look a little sad but sometimes he would be smiling. I think he was remembering the good things about Mom when he was smiling—at least I like to think that.

It could also be that Dad saw Mom in heaven singing with the angels or just resting at the feet of Jesus. But he said the only way she would be able to do that was if everything was picked up and in place, which he was sure it would be. I guess I should tell you that Dad was a preacher, or reverend, and a good one too, from what I've seen of preachers. He stuck to scripture no matter what the issue; if it wasn't in the Word then it was simply just an opinion. This got him into more than one conflict with church leaders when it came to the rules that they set for the congregation.

I do believe he had more faith than anyone I have ever met. I remember the days when we had nothing to eat and not two cents to rub together, but one way or another we were fed and clothed and sheltered. Dad spent a good deal of time on his knees in prayer, but he talked with the Lord throughout the day just the same as he would talk to me or anyone else. More than once I've heard him discussing things with the Almighty as if He were right there next to him—but then again, I guess He was.

It had rained hard for three days straight as we made our way towards our new home and Dad's new commission, a small little mining town back in the hills. Overrun with miners, lumber jacks, teamsters and the rift raft that follows. My father was not a little man by any means and he had a presence about that him that people took notice of when he was around. He loved to laugh and greeted every man, woman or child with a smile, an honest smile. But when he was angry, there was a look in his eyes that would make any man stop and re-evaluate the situation with great concern. I've seen my father step back but I never saw him back down. Maybe that's why he was sent to this place that was full of hard men, doing hard jobs.

But let's get on with the story, it was a rainy spring day that found the Reverend Mr. Black, his son and a wagon stuck in the mud when this big man came walking down the road.

****

The rain had worked its way down to not much more than a drizzle as the gray shadows of dawn began to cast a dim light on the muddy road. The Reverend dug away in front of the wheels as his son stood in front of the two horses hitched to the wagon to make sure they didn't try to move before he was ready. He was muddy and sweaty as he worked away with the shovel.

"Okay son," he said as he stood up and walked to the back of the wagon. "Climb up top there and drive 'em when I give the word. Let's see if we can get this thing rolling. You watch Luke there so he doesn't get away from you."

"Yes sir," the boy answered, knowing that Luke was the younger of the two horses and sometimes got exited.

The twelve-year-old boy climbed up in the wagon seat, unwrapped the reins and waited for his Dad to give the word. The Reverend took a deep breath and then set his shoulder against the wagon to give it a push the from behind.

"Ready?" he asked.

"Yep," the boy answered.

"Okay, get 'em up."

"Get up!" the boy called out to the horses.

The two big horses leaned into their harness as their feet dug into the sloppy mud in an effort to gain some traction. The wagon started to roll but stopped short of coming up out of the hole. They strained at the traces again but the mud would not release its hold or give enough footing to the horses or the man to free it.

"Hold up son!" He called out, then sighed in frustration.

"Whoa!" The boy pulled back on the reins, relieving the horses from their efforts.

"All right Lord," the man wiped his forehead with his arm,

"I really thought that one was going to do it. Maybe you could lend a hand here?"

Just then the Reverend heard the sound of footsteps as they sloshed and sucked in and out of the mud. He turned to see a man coming down the road, and a feeling of relief came over him. Maybe between the two of them they could give the horses enough help to free the stuck wagon. As the man came closer, the Reverend was impressed by the size of the man and smiled at the way God works.

"I asked for a hand but I didn't expect you'd send Samson," he said half out loud. He waited for the man to come within hearing. "Good Morning."

The man walked right on by. He thought it odd that the man did not answer or acknowledge them, maybe he hadn't heard him. "Good morning sir," he said again with the same pleasant smile.

The man hardly turned his head as he cast an unconcerned eye towards the man standing knee deep in mud at the back of the wagon. Without a word he passed by and continued on his way. The Reverend stood in silence and watched the big man leave.

"Well I didn't expect that either," he said, speaking to the Lord again.

"Why didn't he help us out?" the boy asked, looking back at his dad.

"I don't know."

"I guess he ain't the Good Samaritan is he?"

"—isn't the Good Samaritan," correcting the boy's grammar. "And no I guess not. Fact is son, he's probably more like the man beat up and robbed alongside the road."

The boy furrowed his eyebrows at the notion. "I don't think anyone could beat that man up, much less rob him."

The Reverend nodded and then answered. "You'll find that some of the deepest wounds a man receives are on the inside, not on the outside," he looked down the road at the shadowy figure that disappeared into the gray mist of the morning. "You stay put for a minute while I dig out in front of this other wheel, I think that might just get it done."

It was still drizzling rain at ten o'clock when they drove the wagon down the muddy street of the town. Freight wagons were coming and going, being loaded and unloaded while people of all kinds tried their best to stay on the rough cut boardwalks, so that they wouldn't have to trudge through the deep sloppy mud. It really wasn't much of a town as far as towns go, a few stores and twice that many saloons. A livery stable that sat next to the blacksmith shop and a boarding house proper, while numerous shacks and shanties lined the road in and out of the place.

The Reverend pulled up at the stables on the opposite end of town. He climbed down and went into the low-roofed barn to find someone that could help. He walked through the barn and out the other side before he found someone: an old man dumping a wheelbarrow of stall cleanings out back.

"Afternoon sir," the Reverend said.

The old man slowly turned and straightened up, which took a little bit of effort as the pain in his lower back was obvious.

"'Afternoon 'yerself," the old man said with a look of relief at having a reason to rest from his labors. "What can I do you for?"

"Maybe you can point me in the right direction?"

"What direction would that be?"

"I hear tell there's a church around, would that be right?"

The old man gave the preacher a surprised look. "A church? Yeah, there's a church," the old man took off a glove and wiped his forehead with a rag that he took out of his back pocket. "Which way did you come into town, from the north or from the south?"

"We come in from the south."

"Then you need to turn around and head right back the way you come," the old man replaced the worn out rag and then continued. "You know that bridge you crossed 'bout half mile a 'fore town?"

"Yes."

"Well, when you cross it back again, you need to hang a left down a road that ain't much more than a wide path covered with grass. Stay on it 'fer a couple hundred yards 'er so and you'll run right into it if'n you don't stop."

"Thank you."

"If you don't mind me asking," the old man inquired "Why is it you're looking 'fer the church?"

"Because I'll be holding services starting next Sunday. So I guess I better know where the building is at, if I'm going to be preaching. Don't you think?"

"Well I'll be," the old man grinned. "You think there'll be anyone else there 'sides 'yer self?"

"Why certainly," the Reverend smiled back. "There'll be at least five of us there."

"Five?"

"Yep. Me, my boy Mathew, the Father, the Son and the Holy Ghost. And then whatever angels happen to be in attendance, hope there'll be enough room for others when they show."

The old man nodded. "Well, good luck with that. Don't be surprised if the Devil shows up with a few friends also. Hope you fair better than the last fella' that set up shop over there."

"If the good Lords willing, we'll get done what He sent us here to do, whatever that may be. Thank you for your help, we'll see you around I'm sure." The Reverend gave the man a firm handshake and a smile, as he turned to go, he stopped and said, "Oh yeah, one more thing."

"What's that?"

"Is there a job to be had in this town or are they all scraped up?"

"Try the mine," the old man replied. "They go through men at a fairly good rate. Check at the Company store on the other end of town."

"Thank you again!" the Reverend gave him a wave as he left.

The church was made of cut planks nailed parallel to each other with batting at the seams. The boards were gray and weathered, along with being warped and pulled loose here and there. The building was longer than it was wide, with a steep pitched shingled roof, and three steps that led into the front door. There was no steeple or bell or cross to mark the building as being a church, it just sat alone in the middle of a meadow waiting to be used. Off to the right was a two room log cabin with a rock chimney, and a three walled log horse shed next to it. A good size creek ran along the edge of the meadow, the same creek that the bridge crossed over.

The Reverend and his son sat atop the wagon and looked the place over.

"I guess this is it," the Reverend said.

"At least there's shelter for Mark and Luke," the boy offered. "They ain't used to that."

"Aren't. Aren't used to that," correcting the boy gently without looking. "And you're right, they're not used to that; it just might spoil 'em. All right son, let's set up house while we still have the light."

That night they rested beside the fireplace with a cup of coffee. Warming their feet as their boots set nearby to dry, not too close so that they wouldn't dry hard and ruin. Their supper was the very last of the dried corn and jerky, soaked in water and boiled to make a thin stew. But it was good and warm.

"Since I'll be headed to the mine tomorrow, I won't be able to post any flyers in town," the Reverend took a sip of coffee and then continued. "Can I get you to do that for me?"

"I can do it," the boy answered.

"Good. That would be a big help." He was pleased at the willingness of his son to help without complaining. "Tomorrow night we'll have to start cleaning up the church. She still has a good foundation, the walls look to be in good shape, but the roof needs some tending to. Oherwise we'll have a few folks inside that won't be any dryer than if they were outside."

"I saw a stack of shingles in back of the horse shed."

"Good, that will save a lot of time. The Lord has provided the material, we just have to provide the sweat."

"In the sweat of thy face shalt thou eat bread," the boy quoted the scripture without looking to his father.

Once again he was pleased with his boy.

The following morning before daylight, the Reverend wound his watch, started a fire and set last night's coffee over it to heat. This was followed by kneeling in prayer and reading scripture by candle light. After two cups of coffee, he woke the boy before he had to go.

"Remember your prayers and scripture reading before you head out today," he took hold of the door latch to leave. "That is if you want some guidance through the day, otherwise you can just go at it on your own. That's up to you. See to your math studies also, I'll check them tonight. Make sure you turn one horse out at a time and then switch 'em later."

The boy nodded in the middle of a big yawn only half hearing the words his Dad spoke to him. The door closed and he heard his Dad whistling one of his favorite songs as he headed for the mine, the one about a lonesome valley.

Just before the Reverend came to the road that turned off to the mine—a well used rutted quagmire of mud with corduroy bridges strung up and down its whole length—he met up with another man making his way to the mine also. He was a smaller man with a quick, happy step and eyes full of life, an Irishman.

"Good morning to you, friend!" the Reverend called out.

"And a bright fine mornin' it 'tis too!" the little man called out in the dim morning light with a quick wave of his hand.

"I'm sure it is somewhere."

"Tis true, tis true," the Irishman answered back. "Callaghans the name. Clancy Callaghan."

"Black," he answered. "Reverend Black."

"Mother Mary and Joseph," Callaghan replied with a surprise. "The devil won't like that one bit; he's laid a pretty good claim on this here mountain."

"Well, I've been a disappointment to him for quite some time now, so I guess I'll just leave that issue up to the Lord."

"There be more 'n a few folks here 'bouts that don't take to the gospel with open arms, if you know what I mean," Callaghan said with true concern. He was clearly not bashful about speaking his mind.

"Like salt and light. That's what we're supposed to be to the world."

"I'm not sure about the world, but we could sure use a little light down in the mine," Callaghan answered. "But too much salt can ruin the stew, if you know what I mean."

"That's true," the Reverend agreed. "So we'll just use enough salt to season the stew and just enough light to show the path."

Callaghan answered back. "That water into wine thing wouldn't be bad either."

They laughed and talked the rest of the way to the mine, as Callaghan filled him in on what to expect once they got there. He would start out low man on the roll, getting all the dirtiest jobs that needed done. If he made it through that, then he'd have a job tomorrow.

The men that worked the coal mine were as tough as any he had ever seen, right up there with lumberjacks and sailors. Foul mouthed and hard, strong backs and callused hands made up most of the men that went down into the bowels of the earth to dynamite, dig, chip, hammer, and haul out the black chunks of burning rock. It was down in the pit that the Preacher once again saw the man that had passed him on the road when the wagon was stuck.

He looked even bigger down here in the dark with nothing but the lanterns to shed what little light there was. It seemed to him that the man could do more with one swing of a pick or hammer, than any other man could do with three swings. He picked up rocks that no one else could pick up and shoved ore carts about as if they were empty wooden donkey carts. Another thing that struck the Reverend as odd, was that the man never said a word, ever. And no one spoke to him either.

The noon-time break gave them relief from the dark damp confines and from their labors, and even though the sky was still gray from the clouds it was brighter than the cave from which they had come. It was an odd thing to feel the dampness of the mine and yet still breathe in black dry dust from the coal, which they pried from the walls. The air above ground was refreshing to the Reverend's lungs as he took in two long deep breathes. He then proceeded to dump out the sand that had shifted into his boots through the worn-out soles. He dusted off his stockings and then put the worn-out boots back on.

"It looks like they seen better days, ay," Callaghan said.

"Yeah, well, it's not the days that wore 'em out, it was the miles."

"I can relate to that," another miner spoke up. "'Cept' it's my body that's wearing thin, not my boots."

"I hear that!" another added.

"Speaking of getting old," a man named Chris jumped in. "These three old men met up in town one day, and beings it was a very windy day they had a little trouble hearing each other. The first one says to the second, 'It's windy,' to which the second one said, 'No, it's Thursday,' to which the third one said, 'So am I! Let's have a drink!'

The men had a good chuckle and it at least brought a smile to all, except for the big man that sat off by himself.

Callaghan saw that the Reverend had nothing to eat, so he handed him some bread and a chunk of meat.

"Thank you," he said, truly grateful for the meal. He bowed his head, closed his eyes and said a silent prayer of thanks before he ate.

"Next thing you know he'll be preaching," a miner scoffed when he saw him praying.

"Not today," the Reverend replied. "But I will be holding services on Sunday at the church."

That got a few looks from some of the miners, but no one spoke up.

"Oh," he added, "You're all invited, not just my friend here that was requesting a sermon right now."

"I wasn't requestin' nothing," the miner retorted.

"My mistake," the Reverend replied.

"Wait 'till my wife hears this," another miner spoke up. "She's been praying for a preacher ever since the last one left."

"I know where you'll be come Sunday morn," Callaghan laughed.

"Ay, now," Callaghan furrowed his eyebrows and wiped his knuckles across his nose. "I come and go as I please, ain't no woman be telling me."

"Sure you do," the miner laughed along with the others.

Before they had finished with the noon break, the preacher asked Callaghan about the big man.

"Who's that?" he said quietly when the man passed by on his way back down into the mine.

"Names' John," Callaghan answered. "That's 'bout all anybody knows of him. Ceptin' he's strong as an ox, big as one too."

"The bigger they are, the further they have to fall," a young miner spoke up from behind them.

They turned to see who it was and then Callaghan replied. "I wouldn't want to be the man to test that out."

The young man smirked. "Big fellas like that just go through life with people movin' out a their way 'jest 'cause they're big, like a big bull moose in the woods. Hell, most of 'em ain't never even had to fight. They 'jest lumber along with nobody standin' up to 'em at all."

The Reverend could see the young man's ignorance and knew that it would come to no good, but he made no reply. He could see that the boy had probably been in a fight or two but he was talking about things he didn't know. The Preacher opened and closed his fist unconsciously as the memories of his past life slipped back into view. He looked down at the back of his hand and stopped his clenching to stare at the scars on his knuckles.

"I suppose you're a fighter," Callaghan said to the young man. "Been in a lot a' scrapes yourself, I'm guessin'."

"As a matter of fact, I've had my share of tussles and have always come out on top," the young man replied arrogantly.

"Aye, that's the best place to end up," Callaghan affirmed as they stood up from the rocks where he and the Reverend had been seated and headed back to work.

When the young man had walked off ahead of them, Callaghan casually said, "Either that boy ain't never had himself a good wallop or he's just a slow learner."

"With that attitude," the Reverend replied, "I'm sure he'll get another lesson, whether it sticks or not is up to him."

"Aye," Callaghan agreed. "Some people just ain't in the position to learn."

The Reverend looked over at Callaghan. "You're right about that."

****

Mathew made his way into town with a hand full of flyers, a shoeing hammer in his back pocket and a handfull of nails in his front pocket. After stopping to throw a couple rocks and a stick into the creek, he continued down the muddy road as his mind wondered off into the woods. It was a wonder he made it into town at all, but he had a task to do and his father would not be happy if he didn't get it done.

Stopping at the Company store he walked right up and nailed a flyer to the porch post. He stepped back to take a look at his handy work, shrugged and started off.

The door of the store opened up and a man called out, "Hey there!"

Mathew stopped and turned around to see the man looking at him. He looked behind himself to see if the man was talking to someone else, but there was no one else.

"Yeah, you!" the man confirmed.

"Yeah?" Mathew answered.

"You can't just go nailing things up wherever you want!" the man stepped over and tore the paper from the nail. "This is private property and the Company don't tolerate solicitors."

The man looked down at the paper and read it while Mathew stood in the street and waited for whatever was going to happen to happen.

"Oh," the man looked concerned all of a sudden, and a little nervous. "I didn't know it was, ah—I mean, ah, I guess it's all right but you should ask before you go nailing things up all over." The man reached over and pushed the paper back onto the nail. "All right, go on now," he waved the boy off.

Mathew watched the man go back into the store, he shrugged his shoulders and went back to his chore. This time he walked inside the boarding house to ask permission. The man behind the counter was a portly short man with a big black mustache.

"What can I do for you youngster?"

"I was wondering if I could nail this to the post out front?"

"Well that depends on what it is, I guess," the portly man replied. "Let's have a look at it."

He took the paper and read it, as his eyes took in the words they widened and he smiled.

"Well now," he said with a grin as he rubbed the stubble on his chin. "I'm not sure that the folks that make this house their home, are the same ones that will be attending your services, but you're free to post it right out front if you want." He handed the paper back to Mathew and then added, "I've found that guilt will send people to church on Sunday, but desire brings 'em back by Wednesday."

When Mathew was leaving the boarding house a young woman came in. He noticed that she was quite far along with child, her face was downcast and her clothes were worn. She barely lifted her eyes from the floor as they passed. He heard the man behind the counter talking to her as he left.

"I told you to use the back door! Seeing you come and go won't help business any."

"I'm sorry Mr. Hansen," she said softly. "But the back door was locked."

"Agh," he growled. "Well, make sure it's unlocked before you leave next time."

"I did but someone locked it after I left."

"Now why would someone do that?" he grumbled.

"I don't know?" she answered humbly.

That was all that the boy heard, and it didn't make sense to him why the man would make that young lady use the back door, especially when she was with child.

Mathew posted the flyer and then went to the next building and then to the next. No one refused him, but their reactions varied from fear and contempt, to joy and laughter. He noticed another thing also: there weren't any kids in the town. Mostly there were men, young and old, black and white. Then there were some women, not many of them were very old but again they were black and white, a few were dressed nice, but most of them were clothed in well-worn garments.

As he tacked a poster to the wall of another building, a big man stepped out and squinted against the sun light, he was one of the lumberjacks from the near-by lumber camp; a moment later he took notice of the boy next to him. He looked from the boy to the paper he had just placed on the building. He leaned forward to see what it said, glared at Mathew, and then tore the sheet from the wall.

"They don't want this here," he growled.

Mathew took a step back, glancing around and praying for witnesses. When he saw no one, he left the scene as quick as he could. Behind him, he could hear the man wadding up the paper and tossing it to the ground.

After he posted all the flyers, he made his way back to his new home, wandering through the woods along the way. He caught up the loose horse and turned the other out to graze. He stoked up the coals of the fire, and then sat staring at the empty kettle setting there in front of him. He thought about how his dad would handle such situations, he had seen him do it many times. He would just talk to God about it, just like talking to someone as if they were setting right with him. Mathew looked around as if to make sure no one was watching and then he said kind of quiet like.

"Well Lord." It felt awkward. "Ah, I ain't never, ah—I haven't ever just come right out and, ah, talked to you like this, like Dad does. So I'm not sure how this is done and all, so I'm just gonna tell ya' that we ain't got nothing to eat and there's no telling how long it will be 'afore we do. But I guess you know that, so I ain't sure why it is we gotta tell you things that you already know. But Dad says we should pray about everything no matter what, that is, to bring everything to you, so that's what I'm doing. So I guess what I'm saying is, we need something to eat, so that Dad will have strength to work and I can get on with fixen' up the church." He was a little embarrassed about how he had been talking. "Well. I guess that's it. I, ah, I… amen."

He sat and stared at the empty dutch oven, half expecting it to be full at any time and half knowing that it wouldn't. One of the horses whinnied and it brought him out of his daydreams of food. He went to the door and looked down the overgrown road at a wagon coming towards the house with two women sitting up top driving the two horses. Mathew walked out to meet them.

"Hello, young man!" one of the ladies called out—a thin faced woman with black hair pulled back under a bonnet.

"Hello," he answered back as he tipped his floppy hat, just

like he'd seen his Dad do a hundred times.

"I'm Mrs. Talbert," she said, "and this is Mrs. Carter."

The other lady was a little younger with brown hair pulled back in a bun, without a bonnet. She wasn't as thin as the first lady and she was quiet, kind of shy.

"And who is it we would be addressing kind sir?" Mrs. Talbert asked.

"Mathew ma'am," he answered. "Mathew Black."

"The Reverend's boy?" Mrs. Talbert inquired.

"Yes ma'am," he replied.

"Well, come help me down," she ordered him. "Come on," she waved to him as she kept on talking. "You were posting the flyers in town today, seen you at the Company store. Knew right off what needed done."

He hurried over and helped her down out of the wagon and then he helped Mrs. Carter down also.

"Now come back here and help me," Mrs. Talbert said as she let down the tailgate of the wagon. "We've got a few things here to help you and the Reverend settle in," she went on. "I've seen more than one preacher come to town, and unless I'm wrong, you're probably living on hot water and hope. Now you take this here pot and come back for this bundle."

"Yes ma'am," Mathew took the pot and started for the house. He hustled back for the bundle she left sitting in the wagon, and when he picked it up he could smell the hickory smoked seasoning. It was the best thing he had ever smelled in his life.

When he brought it in the cabin, Mrs. Talbert was unpacking a box of dry goods onto the table: coffee, tea, salt, molasses, flour, beans and a loaf of fresh baked bread. Mrs. Carter had brought a broom with her and she was busy sweeping the floor.

"Now you start putting these things away on that shelf right there," Mrs. Talbert pointed and spoke without looking at him.

So he got busy doing what she said and it didn't stop there. He couldn't believe how many things she found for him to do and that was just in the cabin. He did this and that and the other, while the two women buzzed around like two bees. Then all of sudden they were done and she was telling him to help her back into the wagon.

"Come on, help me up now."

He helped her up and Mrs. Carter too.

"You're a good boy Mathew," Mrs. Talbert told him. "You tell the Reverend that we'll see him Sunday if not sooner."

"Yes ma'am. Thank you for everything."

"Think nothing of it," she answered. "It's enough that you've come here to do the Lord's work. God bless you."

Mrs. Talbert took up the reins and swung the team around with as much ease and skill as any teamster, and then headed off down the road leaving Mathew standing there in a daze wondering what had just happened. He scratched his head and watched until they turned the corner and were out of sight. Walking back into the cabin the smell of food washed all over him. But it wasn't the smoked ham; it was something else, something from the fireplace. He walked over and saw the dutchoven swung over the coals with little wisps of steam perking out from under the lid. He lifted the lid with a leather pad and looked inside at the bubbling stew of carrots, potatoes, peas, corn and meat. His mouth watered at the sight of the hot meal. He grabbed a tin plate and scooped some onto it he sat down and ate right then and there. After he had finished what he could get with his spoon, he cut the end off of the bread and mopped up the rest. Then he sat back and in the chair and smiled.

The Reverend didn't get home until dark, but there was a hot meal and fresh coffee waiting for him when he walked in.

He sat down beside the fire and pulled off his worn-out boots, then sat back and closed his eyes. It was then that he realized that there was food cooking over the fire. He looked up at the boy who was standing with a plate of stew,ham and a cup of coffee.

"Where did this come from?"

"We had visitors today," Mathew answered.

"Well, who was it?" he reached up for the plate and cup.

"Mrs. Talbert and Mrs. Carter," the boy replied.

"How'd they know?"

"They seen me posting the flyers today. Mrs. Talbert said she knew right off what needed done, so she and Mrs. Carter came out right away with supplies. She said she's seen more than one preacher come to town with nothin' but hot water and hope."

"Well she's right about that," he got up and went over to the table where Mathew's plate was sitting. "Let's give thanks for this bountiful provisions that the Lord has set before us." He bowed his head, but as soon as Mathew did, he felt guilty because he hadn't giving thanks when he had eaten earlier in the day.

"Lord, we thank thee for providing for us in our time of need. We thank thee for the job you have provided for me and for the good neighbors that you sent to help us. We thank thee for the food that we are about to receive and ask that you would bless it. Guide us and keep us O Lord, I pray these things in Jesus name. Amen."

They enjoyed every single bite of fresh stew and every single sip of fresh coffee. After supper, the Reverend sat by the fire and read the Word, and as always he would read at least one scripture verse, if not a chapter, to his son.

2

The next morning, after prayers and scripture studies, the Reverend headed for the mine and Mathew went to work cleaning up the church. Mrs. Carter had left the broom for him to use and he swept and swept until the whole inside of the one room building was completely full of floating dust. After he had swept and straightened things out a little, he went outside and brought over a bundle of shingles. He just stood there, looking up at the roof wondering what to do next.

"You gonna think them shingles up there?" a voice said.

Mathew jumped and turned around to see an older black man standing there with a canvas bucket, full of tools with a big white-toothed smile.

"How'd you get, ah, where'd you come from?" Mathew stammered.

"Why son, I come from Georgia," he grinned. "Where 'bouts you hail from?"

"I, ah, I'm from ah," Mathew didn't know what to say, he was from a lot of places. "Kentucky, mostly I guess."

"Now that's a shore' sign of a traveling man, it shore' is," the black man laughed. "When a 'fella is mostly from somewhere, he is shore' 'nough from everywhere. Yes sir, now you take my Uncle Jake, yes sir. That man never stayed put more than two months anywhere at any time."

As he kept on talking, he set his tool bucket down and

went over to examine the shingles while Mathew just stood in silence and watched.

"Mama always said, well she said, 'dat man don't stay in one spot long 'nough to cast a shadow,' yes sir that just what she said." He quickly sorted through the shingles as he talked, separating them into two different stacks. "Now Papa, now he kind 'a envied ol' Uncle Jake out there a trapsin' around the country seeing all there was to see, nothing to care 'bout but yer' self and 'yer next meal. I myself think it's a life for the uncommitted type. You know, those folks that don't want people expecting anything from 'em and they don't s'pect nothing from nobody themselves.

"Now you and 'yer Papa is different than that. The whole reason you is travelin' is cause you is doing the Lord's work. That be a whole 'nother reason all together, yes sir. More like the 'postle Paul than Ol' Uncle Jake. Fact is, if a preacher is a traveling it's 'cause he is committed, but you know that. Right?"

He looked up at the dumbstruck boy. "Right?" He repeated. Mathew nodded.

"Now you's wondering how it is I knew you was 'bout to be puttin' shingles up on this here roof. Well the fact of the matter is, I didn't. No sir. I just knew it need some a' them shingles replaced, and when I see'd them posted-up papers in town, well, then I knew right off I better get over here, 'cause if it turns to rain come Sunday you'll have 'yer self some wet folks inside there. So we best get to work." He stood up and looked at the boy with a smile. "You ready?"

"Yes sir."

"Good. If you'll go look off that away behind the cabin, you'll find 'yerself a ladder back off in them tall weeds," he waved him off. "Go on now, fetch up that ladder and we'll get this ol' roof patched up so it don't leak no more. Go on."

Mathew jogged off to fetch the ladder while the man went over and picked up a huge arm load of shingles to sort through again. Not only did he shingle the roof, but he taught the boy how to do it and a lot more besides, for he never did stop talking. But even though he talked on and on, it seemed like there was something to learn in everything he said. A little piece of information here and there that made a person think.

****

The Reverend hefted the rocks into the carts as the sweat streamed down his face amongst the clink and thud of tools that worked against the stubborn earth.

"Hello, John," he said as he passed the big man.

The man glanced over at the Reverend with a look of confusion. John knew he was the same man with the stuck wagon. If the man was speaking to him it must be to goad him for not helping.

The Reverend went on working and didn't say another word to him the rest of the day. At noon he sat with Callaghan again.

"Aye, I see the sun has blessed us with its presence today," Callaghan said.

"It's a beautiful day for sure," the Reverend responded.

"It's a good day for fishing," another miner added.

"Any day's a good day for fishing," said another.

"Amen to that!" the first man replied.

"You know," Chris spoke up, "Speaking of fishing, one time I was fishing with a gent I had just met. I had a boat and he knew the best holes, so we heads up and goes fishing. We'd done real good that morning and were sitting under the High Road Bridge when a funeral procession passed overhead. Well ol' Hardy, that was his name, Hardy. Well he takes off his hat and puts it over his heart real respectful like. I was impressed at the respect he showed and I told him so. I says, 'Hardy.

That's a real honorable thing you done just then for them that was mourning the loss of a loved one.' And Hardy says back to me, 'Well it's the least I could do. I was married to her for thirty years.'"

The others grinned and laughed at the silly tale. All except John, he never smiled.

Soon they were back at work down in the pit with the dust sticking to their sweat-soaked clothes and skin. The Reverend worked as hard, if not harder than most of the men at the mine. No matter what was asked of him, he did it without complaint or hesitation. In an odd sort of way, it felt good to put his back into something hard and see it through. To work side by side with men that were solid; men that didn't back down when things got tough, the kind of men that could look you in the eye. These are the kind of men that set foundations to build on.

****

Before the sun set, the black man had his tools in his bucket and was headed down the road whistling while Mathew waved at his new friend. When the man was out of sight he turned to examine the work they had done. The new shingles stood out against the old ones but it still looked good. The boy was pleased with the finished product and knew his dad would be happy also. As the sun slid down behind the trees, Mathew had a fire going and supper cooking. When his dad walked in, he didn't even sit down.

"All right son, we can't put it off another night. We're going to have to get the church cleaned up and then maybe we can patch the roof on Saturday."

"It's already done," the boy replied.

"What?" the Preacher questioned. "What's done? Did you already clean up in there?"

"Yep," Mathew answered. "And the roof is patched too."

"You replaced the bad shingles?"

"Yep. Well, ah, me and Mr., ah, Mr.—," Mathew realized he didn't even know the man's name. "Dang-it!" he said with disgust.

"What?"

"I don't even know his name."

"Whose name?"

"The man that fixed the roof. He showed me how to set shingles today."

"You don't know who he was or where he was from?" the Reverend asked.

"Nope," Mathew answered. "Dang-it! Oh wait, he said he was from town, 'cause he saw the flyer, but that's all I know."

"Well I'll be," the Reverend said as he stood in the middle of room. "I don't know what to say, I really don't. Thank you son. You don't know what a burden that lifts off my shoulders. Thank you."

"It weren't nothing really," Mathew replied.

The Reverend was just about to correct the boy's English, but thought better of it and let it go. "No. It was something, it really was. Thank you."

He put a firm and loving hand on the boy's shoulder and gave it a squeeze. Mathew was a little embarrassed, but it felt good to have his father's approval.

"Maybe you should do some exploring tomorrow," the Reverend offered between bites.

"What do mean?"

"Go find out what's in those woods out there. Just take off and do some looking around. Wish you had a dog to go with you. But if you want, you can ride old Mark."

"Are you sure?"

"'Course I'm sure."

The next day that's exactly what Mathew did. He took off and explored the woods all day long and the Reverend went back to the mine.

"Good morning John," he said as he walked next to the big man heading down into the mine. "Looks like sunshine again."

John did not reply or even acknowledge the man next to him, but just kept walking in silence with the same expressionless look on his face, as if it were chiseled on stone. With a heavy hammer on his shoulder he walked on. The Reverend said no more at that time, but an opportunity came to him this day. The foreman put him to work with John and the big man did his very best to bury the preacher in his labors. John worked hard and fast trying to get the man behind, but he couldn't quite do it. Just when he would almost have him down the Preacher would find the strength somewhere to catch up, or John would hit a hard spot that would slow him down. When the noon break came John didn't stop, he was going to keep working while the preacher took a break and then he'd have him. But the preacher didn't take a break either; he just kept right at it without a word. The sweat poured from their bodies and soaked their clothes, the dirt and dust stuck to their faces, but they never let up.

When the foreman came by the men taking a break, he heard the hammer down in the pit echoing up the shaft.

"Who's down there?" he growled.

"Aye, that be John and the preacher," Callaghan answered.

"Why they still working?"

"Well now," Callaghan said. "It seems to me that John is bent on burying that preacher down there, but, by heaven, that preacher won't give in or quit."

The foreman stared into the dark tunnel and gave a "humph," then turned and walked away.

Then one of the miners offered up a bet, "I got a dollar says the preacher don't make it to the end of day."

"I got a dollar says he does," Callaghan responded.

"I'll take some of that action if you're willing," another offered. "That preacher can't go at it like that for another half day, a dollar on John."

"I'll take it," Callaghan answered.

The game was on, miners making bets and boasts back and forth, offers and counter offers were laid out. Even the men that didn't usually take part in the betting games joined in.

"You're a fool Callaghan," a miner jeered. "You've worked here long enough to know what John can do. That preacher's a hard worker, there ain't no denying that, but he can't keep up. No way, no how."

"I'm the fool you say?" Callaghan laughed. "You're the one's betting against one of God's anointed."

"Agh," another responded. "That ain't got nothing to do with how hard a man can work. I doubt the Pope could use a shovel well enough to bury his own foot. And he's the anointed of God too."

"Say what you will," Callaghan grinned. "But I'll bet that man down there knew how to work before he ever knew the Lord. Now you put the two together and that's a horse to be betting on."

"Maybe you're in over your head Irishman," the first miner countered. "I don't know the scripture like I should, but I'm thinking it don't favor the gambler none too much. Could be the good Lord won't be pleased with you betting on his anointed servant. Could be he might get upset with you trying to profit off his hard working servant, hmm."

"Well, now, I, ah, I don't think…," Callaghan fumbled around for a response and then he gained some confidence.

"Well now that may be true, so I guess if those of us that is pulling 'fer the preacher to win, then God has looked on us with favor, now hasn't he, and that leaves those of you that was against him in a bad spot I'd say."

"I ain't against the preacher," one miner said with a fearful tone. "I just don't think he can out work ol' John, that's all."

"All I'm saying," Callaghan replied, "is, if the good Lord can part the waters, make the sun stand still and raise the dead, then giving a man a little more strength to finish up a days' work can't be too farfetched. But I could be wrong. I don't think so, but I could be."

"Back to work!" the foreman hollered.

The men headed back down with renewed interest. The ones that had bet on the preacher did little things here and there to try and help without helping, while the ones betting on John made things a little harder in the same way, hindering without hindering.

By noon the Reverend's muscles ached and he knew that not taking a break was probably the best thing, if he would have sat down and relaxed, he would have stiffened up and it would have been harder to get going again. Once he caught his second wind, he really didn't feel too bad, except his feet—the worn out boots no longer let in the sand or even the pebbles, they let in rocks! His feet hurt with every step and he never had a chance to empty them. The only relief was when he could pull the sole away on his left boot and dump the debris out, or when he could shake the pebbles out of the hole in the right boot. But for most of the day he walked on the gravel that collected in them.

But maybe the thing that worked on him the most was the fact that the man they called John, never let up or slowed down. He never once showed any sign of fatigue or the need to rest. This is the thing that not only cast doubts into his mind, of whether or not he could keep up, but it was also the very thing that kept him going. He knew that he couldn't show any signs of being weary either. He knew the game, whichever one of them showed the first sign of being tired, the other man had the edge and it would give that man a little added strength. The Preacher saw this as an opportunity to make an impression on the man. If he could keep up, he knew that John would gain a little respect for him, maybe just enough that he would be able to talk to him, maybe.

And before the day was up the big man had certainly gained a great deal of respect for the preacher, but he didn't let it show. He saw the preacher's worn out boots, he saw him dumping the dirt and gravel out, and he saw that the man never let up either. John saw the bloody hands and scraped up fingers, he saw the sweat soaked, mud caked man that never gave up. Maybe the man was a preacher, but he was also one of the hardest workers he had ever seen.

As they left the mine at the end of the day, the miners made arrangements to settle their debts. The winners laughed and the losers grumbled, but all were impressed with the man that had not only refused to quit, but had actually kept up with the biggest, strongest man in the mine. Maybe there was more to this preacher than just being a bible thumper.

The Reverend and Callaghan walked side by side from the mine, and the Reverend was as tired as he could ever remember being.

Callaghan grinned, "You look like you been pulled through a knothole backwards."

"I feel like it," the Reverend admitted, glad that he had someone to admit it to.

"I don't know if it's a good thing or a bad thing," Callaghan added, "but I don't think you need to worry about having a job at the mine anymore. After today, you can bet they'll be keeping you. Like I said, that may or may not be good from the way you look right now."

"You think there's anything left to mine out of that hole after today?" the Reverend joked backed.

"Aye, I'm sure there's 'nough for tomorrow, but I don't know 'bout the next day," the Irishman was half serious. "There's been talk that it's running out."

"Really?"

"That's the talk."

"It really isn't all that deep is it?"

"Not really, not as far as coal mines go," Callaghan explained. "It started out hot, but it gets weaker and weaker the deeper we go. Could be it will open up again, you never know. The Company has been looking at another area 'bout two miles from here, but they haven't started digging yet."

Just then the two men were startled by the sound of footsteps behind them. They turned to see who it was and were a little surprised to see John. He nodded to the preacher as he passed by. When he was out of hearing Callaghan commented.

"That be the first time I seen him acknowledge anybody, anytime, anywhere. You must have impressed him."

"Probably not the best trade that was ever made," the Reverend replied.

"How's that?" Callaghan asked.

"I impress him and he almost kills me."

The next day the foreman put him back with John again, just for spite. He didn't like the Reverend just because he was that, a reverend.

"He did it one day," the foreman said to one of the miners. "But he can't do it for two."

He made his way down the dark tunnel until he came to where John was getting started. "'Morning John." He didn't expect a reply and he didn't get one.

He set his mind on another hard day but John didn't go at it like he had the day before, perhaps he felt no need to try and put the preacher down. He worked at his normal pace, which was more than anyone else did, but it wasn't the same as yesterday. Maybe John reasoned that the preacher could work and that was an admirable quality in any man.

At the noon break some of the men were still finishing up their debt collecting and making arrangement for payday while the Reverend sat by quietly with his aching feet, but he made no complaints.

"You know," Chris piped up. "I knew a feller' one time had himself a bird that he'd taught to talk."

"Birds can't talk," one miner argued.

"Sure can," another said. "I seen one. They called it a—a parrot. Yeah, that's it.

"You're exactly right," Chris confirmed. "And that's what this bird was. And this feller' was a right good religious boy too, and he'd taught the bird some scripture and he had also tied a string to each leg. So one day a preacher comes along and wants to buy this parrot bird. But he just had to ask about the strings tied to the legs. 'Well,' says this feller,' 'if you pull the right string he'll recite the Lord's Prayer and if you pull the left string he'll recite the 23rd Psalm.' And this here preacher asked, 'What happens if you pull both strings?' at which the parrot squawked 'I'll fall off my perch you idiot!'"

Everyone laughed, except John, who never gave any indication that he had even heard the joke at all. He just got up and went back to work without a word, as usual. The Reverend followed, not wanting to get behind in his work. He finished the day again without falling behind, and he was tired.

Day after day it was the same thing for all of them. Walk into the mine as the sun was starting to rise and walk out of the mine when it was starting to set. Dirty sweat-soaked clothes stuck to their sore muscled bodies. Cuts and bruises were as common as the calluses, which covered their hands. But it was a living; it brought money into the home, put food on the table and clothes on their backs. Some were grateful and some grumbled constantly, but no matter their disposition, they showed up every morning to pry the black stuff out of the earth, then went down to the Company store to pick up whatever cash was left after their store credit was paid off. Sometimes, many times, that wasn't very much, if any at all, and more times than not it was a note of dept.

Saturday evening found the Reverend soaking his feet in the creek when Mathew sat down beside him. "You've done a real fine job around here Mathew. I can't tell you how much it's helped me out not having to worry about the cleaning and fixing that had to be done."

Mathew shrugged, "It wasn't nothing." Just then the boy saw his father's feet through the clear cold creek water. At first he thought it was the water that was making him see things, but upon closer study he could see the cuts and torn flesh on the sides of the feet and he wondered what the bottom must look like. He wanted to ask about it but he wasn't sure how, because it might be embarrassing to his dad, or to himself. The boy picked up the worn out boots and examined the holes that were too large to repair.

"Kind a worn out," he turned one of the boots over in his hand.

"Yep, just a little."

"Are, ah, are you..." the boy was trying to find the words.

"I'm fine," his dad reached over and gave the boy's arm a squeeze. "Don't you worry about it, you hear me?"

Mathew nodded but couldn't stop worrying.

"Let's eat," he quickly pulled his feet from the water, picked up the boots and walked back to cabin. The first few steps were tender.

Mathew sat for a moment; thinking about the cut-up feet. When he started to get up, he saw a smear of blood where his father had stepped. He grimaced at the sight. He kept staring at the blood stained footprints as he stood up but when he turned to leave, he saw something out of the corner of his eye. Across the creek stood the biggest man he had ever seen. The sight of him startled the boy and he took a couple steps back without taking his eyes off of him. The man was just standing there staring at him. Mathew's first thought was to leave immediately, but something told him he wasn't in any danger. Then he recognized him as the same man that had walked past them when their wagon was stuck. The man stood stalk still with a rifle in his hand, which looked too small for him. After a half minute of staring at each other, the big man turned and walked away into the shadows of the forest and was gone.

Mathew said nothing to his dad, thinking it would embarrass him if he knew someone had seen him at the creek.

Sunday morning brought on a drizzle of rain under a gray sky. The Reverend discussed the issue of the weather with the Lord as soon as he heard the pat, pat, pat of the rain dripping off the overhanging limbs and onto the cabin roof. Surrendered to the fact that God would bring to church who he would bring to church, rain or shine, he prepared to deliver the sermon that the Lord had put on his heart, no matter how many or how few showed up.

Looking out across the twelve men, women and children

that came, in-spite of the rain, was a pleasing sight to the Reverend. The Callaghan family was among them, along with Mr. and Mrs. Talbert and Mrs. Carter and her two young children. The black man that had fixed the roof sat in the back, pleased that the room was dry. The Reverend opened up his well-worn Bible, looked out over those attending and smiled at the murmurs, knowing it was probably because of the words carved into the wooden board nailed above the door, which read…

SINNERS ONLY

He began. "There are two kinds of people in this world, sinners and sinners saved by grace. For no one is righteous, not one. All have sinned and have fallen short of the glory of God. We, all like sheep have gone astray. That my dear friends is why Almighty God, Creator of Heaven and Earth, sent His one and only Son to live the perfect life and to then die for the sins of the world, to be resurrected from the dead. The first of the resurrected. To ascend to Heaven to prepare a place for all who will believe in Him and then one day come back in all His glory, Amen.

"We are saved by grace through faith and this not of ourselves. The very faith that saves you, is a gift from God so that no one can boast. God has provided all; He has done it all on your behalf and for His glory, because He loves you with an everlasting love. He has completed the work of salvation on the cross. You can add nothing, nor take nothing from that finished work of grace or it is not finished and therefore it would be worthless to those who are in need of a perfect sacrifice, an unblemished lamb, for the covering of our sins. It is the shed blood of Christ upon the cross that has brought forgiveness of our sins and restoration with God.

"Any attempt by man to add to the way of salvation is to

take away from it. And if you remove one drop of the precious blood of the Lord and Savior Jesus Christ, it is nothing more than a futile attempt to try and make another way, and there is no other way but Christ!

"You either agree with God or you disagree with God. Either you agree that you are a sinner in need of a savior and that Jesus Christ is that Savior and He has paid the price for sin in full or you disagree. It is just that simple…"

The sermon went on with power and praise and when he had finished the man that had fixed the roof slipped out before the Reverend could thank him. The others gathered in the small cabin for something to eat and to get acquainted with each other. The fellowship was good and a long time in coming for the believers in the little community. They were glad that they now had a preacher amongst them, a minister to guide and direct them in the ways of God.

The next morning the Reverend was on his knees in prayer preparing for the day ahead, another day in the mine. And in his prayer he brought up the issue of his worn out boots. Getting up off of his knees he finished his conversation with the Lord.

"I know that you are able and I know that you will provide, but I'm asking that your perfect will and time would be soon. My feet are hurting Lord, and it's not that I'm asking for sandals that never wear out, but I am asking for another pair of boots. Used is fine, as long as they don't have any holes. But you know all this and I'll not bring it up again, at least not until I get to the mine." He opened his Bible and sat beside the fire, sipping his coffee until it was time to wake Mathew and head out.

"Good morning John," he said when he met the big man walking to the mine.

"'Morning," John replied.

The Reverend took three more steps before it dawned on him that the man had just answered his greeting. By then John was several steps ahead of him, he wanted to run up and keep talking, but he knew better and it was all he could do to keep from it. He reasoned with himself and realized that it was just a simple early morning greeting that goes on all over the world every day, and it really wasn't that big of a deal. But his spirit told him it was the little seeds that produced much. He smiled to himself and found renewed strength in his work.

At noon the men were all seated at their same places talking and eating like always, and again, Chris had another joke to share.

"Say, Callaghan," he called out. "Here's a little known fact I'll question you on."

Callaghan looked up.

"Which side of a chicken has the most feathers?"

Callaghan furrowed his eyebrows in deep thought while the other miners thought on the question as well. "I don't know that one side would have any more or less feathers than the other, at least not that you could say so on every chicken."

"Then you'd be wrong, my friend, because the fact of the matter is, every single chicken that ever hatched from an egg has more feathers on the outside."

The men that had not thought of the answer grinned at how obvious the answer had been.

"You know," Chris went on. "Speaking of cooking, (which they weren't), that reminds me of a conversation that I overheard between my Aunt and Uncle. We were settin' down to a nice beef steak dinner when Aunt Paula (that was her name, Aunt Paula named after Grandma Paula), well Aunt Paula says to Uncle Frank, 'back when we was first married you used to take the small piece of steak and give me the larger one. You don't love me no more.' At which Uncle Frank replied, 'Nonsense, my dear. You're just a better cook now."

The men enjoyed the humor and a good laugh.

"Will you join us in town tonight Preacher?" Chris asked.

"What's going on in town tonight?"

"Same as any other night," Chris replied. "We get together for a beer or two. Sit and talk. Relax a little. You in?"

"Aye," Callaghan added. "Come join us."

"All right," the Reverend answered. "I'd be glad to join you."

"Good," Chris responded. "We'd be glad to have you."

3

The Reverend walked into the smoky room and stood for a moment to allow his eyes time to adjust to the dim light. He saw Chris give a wave from the back of the tavern. He acknowledged the wave and started weaving his way through the tables towards the men waiting for him.

"Didn't know if you'd come," Chris waved to the bar for someone to come over.

Callaghan slapped the table. "Aye, he said he was coming did he not? Why would ya' doubt it?"

"You never know," Chris shrugged.

The Reverend looked around the room at the men that filled it up. He recognized the miners and it wasn't hard to pick out the lumberjacks from the clothes they wore: tall, lace-up boots with their trousers tucked in or cut off (so that the loose bottoms wouldn't catch on the limbs and trip them). Some of the men were loud and some sat silent. Some were playing cards and some were just drinking. Laughter was heard from all corners of the smoky haven, and the smell of beer was not missing either.

"I got'a tell 'ya," Chris leaned forward a little. "I didn't know preachers could work that hard."

"Is there any other kind of work?" the Reverend grinned.

"Not that I ever found," Chris replied.

"Me either," Callaghan added.

"It's the only way I know how to work," the Reverend continued, "My Dad wouldn't have it any other way. He figured the good Lord put the sun in the sky to give us light to work by. So we did, my brothers and I and my sisters too. We worked from can to can't. From wh—"

"—when you can see to when you can't." Chris finished the sentence.

"That's it," the Reverend agreed as the three men laughed.

"Me father would work us like we was mules," explained Callaghan. "Then we'd drink like we was fish, fight like we was dogs, and then sleep like we was babies," the Irishman lifted his glass for a toast. "May the Lord protect my tomorrow as he did my yesterday."

"Here, here!" the Reverend agreed.

"Skoal," added Chris as they all drank to the toast and then he said. "You know, that reminds me of Mr. and Mrs. Murphy."

"Good Lord," Callaghan said. "Here we go."

Chris went on without missing a beat. "You see, old man Murphy had himself a drinking problem—at least Mrs. Murphy thought so. Well Mrs. Murphy got herself some advice from a friend on how to put a stop to him spending so much time at the pub and coming home so late. She tells Mrs. Murphy that because he comes home through the cemetery every night, that she should disguise herself and spook him when he comes staggering through. So Mrs. Murphy does just that, and when old man Murphy came by she jumped out and startled him. To which he said, "Who are you?" To which Mrs. Murphy replied. "I'm the devil!" To which Mr. Murphy responded by shaking her hand and saying, "Glad to finally meet you, I'm your brother-in-law."

In the middle of sharing a good laugh at the joke, the doors slammed open and in walked the young miner that thought himself a fighter, and by the way he came in with his three friends, he was looking for one tonight. He stood in the doorway and looked about the room with arrogance, a look of challenge and defiance. The men in the tavern took little notice and went back to their conversations.

"Carter," Chris said with a tone of disgust.

"Him?" the Reverend asked.

"Yeah," Chris replied. "Jackson Carter. Poor kid thinks he's got something to prove all the time."

"Carter, Carter," the Reverend repeated the name. "I had a young woman come to Sunday service by the name of Carter would she be…"

"Two kids?" Chris asked.

"Yes, a boy and a girl."

"His wife," Chris shook his head. "He married a whole lot better than she did."

"That be true," Callaghan added. "She's a fine young lady 'tis true. And that young bull 'jest keeps pawing at the dirt and kicking' up dust."

"Trying to prove he's a man," the Reverend said.

For the next half hour or so things were pretty much the same, but then young Carter had enough drink in him to encourage his efforts of being tough. He got louder and more belligerent with every minute. It was obvious that the other men were annoyed but they all hoped he would simply shut up or leave. When he began directing his comments directly at some of the others, the men still ignored him, which made him try all the harder. He was bound and determined to have himself a fight.

Chris shook his head. "His bullfrog mouth is 'gonna overload his humming bird a…, uh, butt."

"Yep," the Reverend said. "I best be heading for home."

"Ah," Callaghan frowned. "Don't be letting that kid ruin a good evening."

"Not at all, it's just time to go is all."

"Well, thanks for joining us," Chris said with a smile.

"My pleasure, we'll see you boys in the morning."

"See ya tomorrow Preacher," Callaghan waved.

As the he made his way to the door it happened, the very thing he didn't want to happen happened.

"Hey preacher man!" Jackson Carter called out.

The Reverend tensed at the words but tried to hide it. He turned with a smile and looked over at the young man.

"What's the matter? Can't hold up with the real men?" Jackson and his two friends laughed. "The night's still young and 'yer headed home. Could be the drinks too strong and the language too coarse for a preacher, uh?"

The Reverend nodded and grinned. "Yep, that's it. You young'uns can burn both ends of the candle, but not me."

Jackson started walking towards him. "Little too rough 'round these parts uh? Maybe you should take up quiltin' with the ladies instead of trying to stay up with the men."

"Quilting?" the Reverend nodded. "I'll have to think on that but I'm not sure that I've got the skill, nor the patience for quilting."

Jackson stopped directly in front of him and gave the Reverend a hard look. "You don't belong in here with real men, preacher. Maybe you best go home."

For some unknown reason the Reverend all of a sudden found the whole thing funny. He grinned. "Now that my friend, is some good advice and that's just where I am headed."

He smiled and winked at the strutting rooster, then turned and walked away. This made the man even angrier, and as the Reverend was headed for the door, the young miner quickly walked over to a nearby table and picked up an empty mug and threw. The Reverend saw it from the corner of his eye and ducked as it passed over his head and crashed into the corner of the tavern. The Reverend straightened up and glared at the man with a look that said, 'you've gone too far.'

But Jackson Carter wasn't looking at him and neither were his friends. They were looking past him to where the mug had landed, and so was everyone else. The Reverend turned slowly to see what everyone was looking at. Back in the shadows of the tavern wall, a shadow stood up, towering over everyone and everything. John walked across the room with slow and powerful strides; passing by the preacher without a glance he walked directly up to Jackson with that cold chiseled look on his face.

At first Jackson was taken back, but his pride quickly got the better of him and he sneered at the approaching man.

"All right then. You don't scare me like you do these others. I'll take you down right here and now!"

John didn't say a word; he just stood and stared at the young miner. For a moment everything was as still and quiet as a coffin and then Jackson hauled off and hit John with everything he had. His right fist struck the man in the side of the head with a thud. John's head had barely moved, then he slammed his open hand into Jackson's chest, knocking him backwards ten feet and into a table. With a quickness and smoothness that surprised everyone, John was immediately standing over the fallen man, lifting him off the wooden floor by his shirt. Jackson was trying to catch his breath but he couldn't, his mouth gapped like a fish out of water but no air would come in. The big man threw him against a log pillar. The young brash, tough talking miner's body went limp as it hit the floor. John walked up and stood over him for a moment, then turned and left the tavern, passing the Reverend without a glance.

The Reverend went over to see how bad the man was hurt. Right away you could see that he was unconscious with a broken left arm.

The men gathered around with their comments on how stupid the man was in the first place and what short work John had made of him in the second place.

"Maybe he'll think twice before he goes to throwing things around next time," one commented.

"Or he'll take better aim," another offered.

"Keeping his mouth shut would go a long ways in preventing things like this," Chris added.

"That be true enough," Callaghan agreed.

The Reverend stood up and shook his head. "Will you two help me get him home?" he asked Chris and Callaghan.

Chris gave him an odd look. "You 'gonna help him after the way he treated you?"

"Yep."

Chris shook his head. "All right, but it don't make a lick o' sense to me. You ought 'a be the last person to help him out, ought 'a let him lay."

"Give me a hand," the Reverend ignored the statement as they lifted the unconscious man. "Is there a doctor anywhere around?"

"Company doctor," someone answered.

"Good," the Preacher replied. "Will someone go get him and send him to the Carter home?"

For a moment no one answered, but then a lumberjack spoke up, a big man sitting at a table with several others. "You bleedin' heart do-gooder, leave him be. This is a tough country and only the tough deserve to live here. The week and feeble die or go home. That loud mouth wimp got what he was askin'

50

for, so stay out of our affairs or you'll get the same."

The Reverend stopped and let his eyes fall hard on the lumberman. Neither man showed any fear, and they both saw it in the other.

"We never asked for a preacher, or a church," the lumberjack said, "that's for the weak and helpless. You should 'a stayed on the other side of the mountain, 'cause this is where the devil lives. Welcome to purgatory."

The Reverend never flinched as his eyes remained on the man; finally, the lumberjack looked away with a sarcastic grin and drained his mug of beer, only then did he remove his stare.

"Will someone go for the doctor?" he asked again.

"I'll do it," someone finally answered. His eyes cut across the room at the lumbermen as he stood up to leave.

"Thank you, I appreciate it." The three men proceeded out of the tavern with the unconscious man; another man stepped in and grabbed a leg to help.

When the preacher and the others had left the tavern, the lumberjack shot another glance at the door before returning to his card game and a whiskey.

"So Murphy," one of the men at the table spoke up as he laid down a card. "I take it you don't much care for that preacher man."

Murphy McAlister leaned over and spit tobacco juice onto the floor. "You got that right."

"Why's that?" another asked.

"Don't need a reason to dislike someone," he answered. "But in this case, it's because I know his kind. Don't fool yourself; they're against men like us and everything we do." He picked up his shot glass and drained it. "They'll sit in that little excuse of a church and condemn us to hell all day long. Believe me, it won't be long before they're shutting down the boarding house, then the gambling will be shunned and then the taverns themselves will close. Mark my words."

"It's one little church with no more than half a dozen folks showing up," the first man replied. "They ain't got no more say-so than a mule."

"Huh," Murphy responded with a smirk. "You'll see. If that preacher man sticks around things will change; that's what they do, change things."

When Jackson Carter came to, he was in a great deal of pain. He could not breathe without terrible suffering in his chest, which kept his breathing extremely shallow. His head throbbed horribly and his left arm ached just as bad. When his vision cleared, he saw his wife next to him holding his hand. He blinked in an effort to clear his mind as well as his vision and then asked.

"What happened?"

"The doctor says you'll be all right, but it'll be a while," his wife answered. "Your arm is broke."

"My ribs hurt bad," he groaned.

"We didn't know how bad they'd be," she replied.

"You took a pretty good whack," the Reverend was standing off to the side.

"Who's that?" Jackson questioned with an obvious look of pain.

"The Reverend brought you home," she answered.

"What for?" Jackson grimaced as the pain in his side stabbed at him and the memory of what he had done started coming back.

His wife's lips tightened and her eyes narrowed. "Because you weren't able to do it on your own."

Jackson was angry and embarrassed but kept his comments to himself, for once.

The Reverend walked up to the bed with his hat in his hand. "The doctor was worried about those ribs, bruised at the least, but probably broken. Like getting kicked by a mule. He'll be by tomorrow to check on you. I've got to be going, just wanted to make sure you came out of it all right. I'm afraid you'll be laid up for awhile with that arm and the ribs."

He saw the worried look on the young woman's face as the thought of her children and no money for food came to mind. She followed the Reverend to the door.

Knowing the young man's pride, he whispered to her. "It'll be all right, try not to worry too much; the Lord will meet your needs."

She forced a smile. "Thank you Reverend."

The incident was talked about all morning at the mine and no one was surprised that Carter wasn't there. The preacher was a point of topic also; because of what he had done for the man, although the Reverend himself added little to the conversations. One man said that he had seen John get into a fight once before, when he had been working down south.

"I seen him down Louisiana way, some years back," he began, "had some kind 'a trouble over a Cajun woman down there. Big fella' called John out to settle the matter." He paused, but then went on. "Carter better thank God he ain't dead 'cause that 'fella down in Nor'leans shor' got dead, and it didn't take but one big right hand to make him that way."

"Killed him?" A miner asked.

"Yep. That's the long and short of it. That big 'fella hit John and then he hit the floor with his scull caved in."

"Not too hard to imagine," Callaghan said.

After a moment of silence Chris just couldn't resist another story. "You know, that reminds me of the time my Uncle Harman found himself down in Louisiana with a little extra money on his hands. Well now, he had seen a fella walking around with some of them there alligator shoes on, and my-oh-my did he think they was sharp. So he found a man that sold them shoes; but lord a mercy, that man liked them shoes more than Uncle Harmon did 'cause the price was as high as a healthy pine. So Uncle Harmon tells that man that he can keep them shoes 'cause he's gonna go fetch himself a 'gator' and make his own pair of shoes. To which the shoe man replied, 'Go ahead, but watch out for them two 'ol boys down on the Bayou doing the very same thing.' So Uncle Harmon gets all head up and goes down to the Bayou his self. Now, as he's a poling along he sees two stout young men standing in the water, real still like, holding clubs. Just then Uncle Harmon sees a gator coming at 'em and he thinks to his self, 'self, this is gonna be something to see.' Now that gator moved in nice and easy like, and them boys stood stalk still until it looked like that big ol gator was just about to take a bite and then WHAM, they clubbed that gator good right upside his head. Knocked him goofy but it didn't knock him out, no sir. But I guess that didn't matter to those two boys 'cause they just jumped right on ol' Mr. Gator and wrestled him up on the bank where they gave him another good clubbing. At which point Uncle Harmon noticed that there were at least three or four other gators a lying on the bank. Then they rolled the gator over and threw up their arms in disgust and exclaimed. "Why this 'un ain't got no shoes neither!"

While the others enjoyed the story John never even cracked a grin.

The week went by just about the same as the week before. Early to the mine and late to go home, sweat and dirt mixed with muscle and grit was the miner's life. But on Saturday evening, the Reverend took Mathew and headed to town and the Company store for supplies. Boots were on the list, but they would have to wait. He and Mathew went straight in and bought food staples enough for two adults and two kids.

When they left the store, a commotion down the street caught their attention. Out in front of the tavern a small crowd had gathered. His first instinct was to take Mathew and leave, but something inside compelled him to investigate. With a sigh he headed down the street.

He could see between the people gathered around, that a man was on the ground and another man was standing over him. As they got closer he could see that the man standing was the lumberjack, Murphy McAlister.

"This won't be good," he whispered to himself.

Mathew stayed close behind his father as they excused their way between several onlookers. Once inside the circle, they saw that the man on the ground had blood running from his nose and a cut above his eye. He pushed himself up to his knees and spit some blood out on the ground. With a reluctant effort, he stood up and faced the big man again, who was grinning with arrogance and triumph.

The bleeding man wiped the blood from his face. "I didn't cheat you." He looked at the blood on his arm. "You're just not very good at cards."

Murphy's big fist came down onto the left side of the man's face, which drove him down to the ground once more. But this time Murphy stepped up and kicked the man in the ribs; forcing a rush of air from the man's lungs, along with a groan. Then the big man kicked him again and again and again. His face showed anger mixed with pleasure as he delivered blow after blow, until a strong voice from the crowd spoke up.

"That's enough," the Reverend's voice was stern and uncompromising.

Murphy stopped and slowly looked up from the moaning man on the ground to the man that had interfered.

"This ain't none of your affair, Preacher."

The Reverend nodded, "He's had enough. I don't know what your disagreement is about, that's true. But whatever it was, it's over now. I'm sure he's paid up for any insult he might have made against you."

Murphy clenched his teeth and took a deep breath, flaring his nostrils like an old bull. He glared at the preacher as the muscles twitched in his jaw and his fists clenched white. The Reverend Black stood stalk still with an armload of packages and a dead calm stare in his eyes. It was a look of assurance, courage and absolutely no fear and Murphy saw it. He was sure he could whip the preacher, but it wouldn't be easy. All he needed was one good shot and he'd lay the man out cold. His fists worked even tighter. The preacher was standing on the other side of the groaning man on the ground; it was just half a step too far for him to land a good stout punch. He felt a hand on his arm and far off voice.

"Come on Murph," the voice urged, "leave it be. Let's go back inside, come on."

Murphy glanced at the man who had a hold of his arm and then looked back at the preacher. The man at his arm kept up the urging while the preacher in front of him never flinched or moved, but simply stared him square in the eye.

The Reverend knew he should look away and not keep his eyes fixed on the man, but he couldn't move them away. The man was a bully and not one to bluff. He liked to fight, that was plain to see, and the tougher the opponent the better. He knew that the man wanted nothing more than to land that big right hammer of a fist up alongside his head. This man had run people over his whole life and that made the Reverend even madder.

He'd fought men like this before, back in his younger days, back before he began serving the Lord. He'd fought them and won, and he knew he could win this fight too. But something tugged at his conscience, pulled at his mind that he was not led here to this time and place to fight with his fists. He pushed the thought aside and calculated just what he would do if Murphy took a swing at him. It would be justified, and no one could speak ill of him for protecting the beaten man on the ground.

Murphy looked past the preacher into the crowd behind him and could see in their faces that they were siding with the preacher and against him; he hated the man in front of him even more. The man at his arm pulled and urged him to walk away, but Murphy wanted nothing more than to hit the preacher right square in the face. Eventually, he backed away and returned to the tavern with one last glance of hatred at the preacher.

As the two men disappeared into the tavern, the Reverend watched for another few seconds before turning his attention to the man on the ground who was struggling to his feet.

"Are you okay?" he asked.

"No one asked for your help," the man replied as he spat blood out onto the ground and then wiped his mouth.

"I was just trying to help."

"Well, you didn't help anything," the bleeding man answered. "I'll never hear the end of it, that a preacher stepped in to stop this thing. You didn't help at all." He never looked at him, just walked away wiping the blood from his face.

As the people began dispersing from the scene, they began talking and what they said let the Reverend know that this probably wouldn't be the end of the matter.

"Never thought I'd see Murphy back down to anyone."

"Me either. But if the preacher hadn't stepped in, he might have killed that man."

"I wonder what that preacher would have done if 'ol Murph' would have laid one on him?"

"I'd pay to see that fight."

"You think he'd fight back?"

"Be a fool if he didn't. He'd take a beatin' worst than that other man did."

As they were walking towards the Carter home, Mathew brought up the boots, he wanted to talk about the incident with the lumberjack, but thought he better not.

"Why didn't you get some boots?"

"Maybe next week."

"But you had the money today. You could 'a got 'yer self some new ones even."

The Reverend smiled and gave the boys' head a good rub. "Your right, I could have. But that's not what the Lord wanted me to do. This is a better thing that we're doing; better than a new pair of boots."

"How do you know?" Mathew pried.

"That it's a better thing?"

"Yeah, well, no, I mean, how do you know it's what God wants you to do?" Mathew was perplexed and a little upset that his dad hadn't bought the boots.

"That's a good question son. Most folks never ask that question, much less take any time to find the answer. You see it's like this: when you become a child of God, then God's very own spirit comes to dwell within you—that is, He comes to live inside of you. Your old dead spirit is born again and made alive in Christ and from that point on; you begin to have a relationship with God. He walks with you and talks with you and you have communion with the Creator of the universe. Now the more you pray and the more you read the scripture and the more you fellowship with other believers, the more clear God's voice will come to you," he then quoted, "And when he putteth forth his own sheep, he goeth before them, and the sheep follow him: for they know his voice."

"Does he talk out loud to you?"

"Well, sort of," the Reverend thought for a moment. "I guess you could say that I can hear him with my inner ear. Some say it's your conscience, that little voice inside of you that tries to talk you out of mischief. You've heard that voice, haven't you?"

Mathew nodded.

"Although I have met some that say the Lord has spoken out loud to them just the same as I'm speaking to you. I sure wouldn't question it."

They walked along in silence, both of them pondering the conversation. Mathew rolled the words of his father around in his head, and the Preacher wondered if he had said the right things, in the right way.

The soft glow of light though the window could be seen long before they reached the heavy wooden door. After a solid knock, it only took a few seconds for the latch on the other side to be slide away and the door to be cracked open. Mrs. Carter peeked out through the slight opening to see who it was.

"Reverend?" she said with surprise. "What are you doing here?"

"We just stopped by to drop off a few things that you might need," he held up the groceries with a pleasant smile.

"Please come in."

"No, that's all right, we don't want to disturb you," he replied.

"No, please, please come in." She insisted with a look that could not be denied.

"Very well," they walked in with the groceries to see the two Carter children standing shyly beside their dad, staring at the visitors with interest.

"Jackson," Mrs. Carter said happily, "the Reverend has come to call."

The young man sat in a chair beside the fireplace. He grumbled and frowned at the sight of the Reverend.

"How're you feeling, Mr. Carter?" the Reverend set the supplies on the table.

"I'm all right," the man grumbled, eyeing the Reverend's load with interest. "What's in those?"

"Just a few extra groceries that have been donated. Figured you might be able to use them."

"We can get along just fine without any handouts," Jackson frowned.

"Jackson!" Mrs. Carter scolded her husband with a glare.

"Oh, no doubt," the Reverend replied. "It's not so much of a handout as it is just a helping hand. Thought it might help in the healing process if you had a sack of beans in cupboard. That's all."

"Thank you so much Reverend," she pleaded her apology. "We really do appreciate it. Really."

"Thank the good Lord for providing Mrs. Carter," he answered.

"We do," she replied.

"We'll let you alone and be on our way," the Reverend said. "Let me know if there is anything I can do for you. Good evening Mr. Carter, Mrs. Carter, kids." He smiled and gave the kids a wink.

"Thank you so much," Mrs. Carter said yet again, grasping the preacher's hand sincerely.

****

There were fifteen people at Sunday service, and once again the roofer came and went before the Preacher could thank him. The fellowship afterwards was sincere and full of laughter. The people stayed longer and were forming new and stronger friendships. Mrs. Carter attended with her two children. She asked Mrs. Talbert whom she should thank for the food that the Reverend had brought by. Mrs. Talbert said that she knew nothing about it, but that she would look into it. When everyone had gone and Mr. and Mrs. Talbert were getting ready to go she walked casually up to the Reverend and asked flat out.

"Who do we need to thank for providing the Carters with groceries?"

He answered without hesitation or stumbling over words. "I gave my word not to say, the contributors wish to stay unknown but I will pass on the thank you."

Mrs. Talbert studied the Reverend's face and then nodded. "You just do that for me."

He smiled and helped her into the wagon. "Thank you for coming Mr. Talbert, Mrs. Talbert."

"Fine sermon, Preacher," Mr. Talbert called out with his dry monotone voice. "Reckon I'll be back next week for more."

"Glad to hear it," the Reverend called back as their wagon rocked and bumped its way down the road.

The next day, the Reverend was working alongside John once more and they were drilling in order to set charges, which meant that one man held the drill rod and the other man swung the hammer. With every swing of the hammer, the holder would give the drill a quarter turn. It was a dangerous job, for the holder.

From out of the dark tunnel came the methodic ring of hammer driving steel.

'Clink...clink...clink...clink'

"Your turn," John said, holding the hammer out for the Reverend to take.

The Reverend hesitated for a second, wanting to explain that he had not hammered a drill before, but realized that John already knew it.

"All right." He took the heavy steel hammer, set it on top of the drill bit head and tapped it once. When he heard the satisfying chink, he raised the hammer a little higher and tapped it again, then again, each swing was a bit more confident than the last. In a short time he was ringing the steel with good solid swings, John never once looked up.

As they headed out of the mine that evening, John spoke up from out of the blue.

"Why'd you help that man?"

The Reverend wasn't as surprised as he thought he would be, but that may have just been because he was tired. He thought about it for a second, it was almost the same question as Mathew had asked him.

"Seems odd, huh," he replied, and then thought a moment more before continuing. "He's an angry young man with a chip on his shoulder and something to prove. No reason his family should have to suffer for it." He paused and then admitted, "But even if he didn't have a family, I still would've done it."

"Why?"

"Because that's what the Lord asked me to do."

"That don't make sense," John stated flatly.

"Not to the worlds way of thinking, it doesn't," the Reverend agreed, "but if the Lord reached down to me, how can I not reach out to another?"

They walked along in silence while the Reverend kept trying to think of something else to say, but nothing came to mind, so he simply walked beside the man....and prayed in silence.

The next day was a let-down for the Reverend; he was looking forward to working with John. Because they were blasting, the foreman sent him into town with Mr. Talbert, one of the mines teamsters, to bring back a load of timbers. Mr. Talbert was not much of a talker, so the ride was a quiet one.

"Ever been to Texas?" Talbert asked, quite a while into their journey.

"No, I haven't," he answered, expecting the man to go on and tell him about it. But he didn't. In fact, he never brought it up again. The Reverend waited and then shrugged it off.

"This here is a good team," Talbert said later. "Not the best, but good."

"How long have you been driving?" He questioned, thinking they were going to strike up a conversation.

"All my life," Talbert replied, before falling into silence again.

As they made their way through town, the Reverend purposely took notice of all the people that he saw and tried to study their faces, young or old, men or women. One young woman in particular caught his attention, for she was with child and walked with her face downcast. But as they passed the livery, he looked into the open doors of the barn and saw Mathew. It looked like the boy was cleaning stalls. He had the urge to go see what he was up to, but decided it could wait until that evening.

When the timbers were loaded and delivered to the mine, Talbert climbed back onto the wagon and said, "Thanks Preacher, it's been nice visiting with 'ya." And then he drove off. The Reverend scratched his head and grinned at the man's odd character.

That night after supper, while they sat by the fire, the Reverend inquired about what Mathew had been doing that day. "I saw you in town."

Mathew was surprised. "I thought you was at the mine?"

"—'were' at the mine," he corrected him. "And I was, but they sent me to town with Mr. Talbert to fetch back some timbers. What were you doing?"

"Working," Mathew answered in a matter-of-fact way.

"At the livery?"

"Yep, Mr. Sommers hired me on. Said things was busy now and he could use another hand."

"You don't have to if you don't want to," he was worried that the young boy was fretting about their situation too much.

"I know it," Mathew answered. "But I want to, if it's okay."

"It's all right with me. It sure won't hurt you none to be busy, and it will give you a little spending money besides."

"That's what I was thinking. I s'pose I should 'a asked you first."

"That might have been wise," the Reverend replied. "But I think it's all right. You be sure to work hard for Mr. Sommers."

"I will," the boy answered with assurance. "I will."

"I have no doubt."

The next day everyone was hauling rocks out of the mine from the blasting. That evening, the Reverend was once more soaking his feet in the cold creek. And the day after that the miners went back to work with picks hammers and shovels, hauling rocks and building supports with the timbers. Only the conversation of the men truly changed the landscape of their surroundings. A story here, sarcasm there, and a joke from Chris would always bring a laugh to everyone. Well, almost everyone.

****

There were twenty people at the church on Sunday. The Reverend was pleased with what the Lord was doing. But today when his roofer entered the church before the service, he walked back and stuck out his hand for the black man to shake.

"Good morning, sir," the Reverend said with a smile.

"Morning, Reverend," the man grinned back, a little embarrassed by the attention he was getting.

"I apologize for this, but you left me no choice," the Reverend went on. "I was obligated to at least thank the man who fixed the roof on the Lord's house. And I was bound and determined to shake his hand."

"No thanks necessary Reverend," the man replied. "No thanks needed. No sir. I's happy to do it. Fact is it should a' been done long a 'fore, so I apologize for putting it off."

"May I ask your name sir?"

"Mr. James, sir. Edward James."

"It is a pleasure to finally meet you Mr. James. I hope you will stay after the service and join us for dinner. There'll be plenty and we would certainly enjoy your company."

"I don't want 'a be a bother," he said.

"No bother, glad to have you." The Reverend nodded a confirmation and then went back to the front of the church and began the service.

"And God said let there be light and there was light,

And God said unto them be fruitful and multiply and replenish the earth and subdue it,

And God said unto Noah,

And God said unto Abraham,

And God said unto Jacob,

And God said unto Moses,

And God said unto…You.

That's right, God has spoken unto you and more than that, he is speaking to you this very day. Through His Word and through the foolishness of preaching and through the very creation that surrounds you; God Himself, is speaking to you. And even more than that, is the fact that if you have been saved by believing in the name of Jesus Christ, then it is the very Spirit of God that resides within you, to teach you and guide you. It is the very Word of God that has been written upon your heart. God is speaking but are you listening? God is calling unto you, but are you answering Him? ...."

Outside, at the edge of the meadow, stood a man in the shadows listening to the words that the Reverend Black was speaking. The big man pondered the words with a great deal of doubt and skepticism, but he found himself compelled to hear it out. The Preacher was unlike any other man he had ever met, or even heard of. He wanted to see, or at least hear, for himself, if he was the same man within the walls of the church as he was within the walls of the mine. If nothing else, John was curious as to why a man would act in such foolish ways as this man did.

After the service, the Reverend asked Mrs. Talbert about the young woman he had seen in town. She may not know but the town wasn't all that big and how many women could be with child, so it was worth asking. He wasn't sure why he needed to know, but he was led to inquire.

"Molly Miguire," Mrs. Talbert said with a raised eyebrow and a hushed tone, "works at the boarding house, that is until she became with child. They keep her busy still, I guess, but at more…how should I say…more respectable duties than before. But if she is anything like the other girls that work there, she'll be back to her former duties after the child is born."

"What kind of person is she?"

"What do you mean 'what kind of person is she?'" Mrs. Talbert questioned back. "I just told you."

"Mm, yes, I suppose you did," the Reverend nodded. "But is she a mean woman or is she kind? Is she a harsh person or a gentle person? Does she long for something better or is she satisfied with her position in life? Does she want for change or is she content? I guess that's what I mean when I asked what kind of person is she."

"Oh, I,I…" Mrs. Talbert stuttered. "I don't know. I, ah, I truly don't know Reverend, I'm sorry."

"Nothing to be sorry for Mrs. Talbert. No reason you should know such things about the woman."

"Maybe not," she answered with humility. "But I had already decided, and for that I am sorry."

"God bless you Mrs. Talbert," the Reverend said with a tender smile.

The next evening, after leaving the mine, the Reverend had Mathew meet him at the mining road turn off, and together they went to town to call on some of the folks that had attended church. As they walked down the boardwalk in the fading light of day, the Reverend greeted everyone with a smile and called them by name, if he could. Mathew couldn't help but notice the new pair of boots that sat in the window of the Company store, and he longed to have enough money to buy them for his dad. He had even gone into the Company store and picked them out. But it was going to take much longer than he wanted before he would have enough money to buy them.

Tacked onto a few store fronts and posts, they saw a notice that called for a town council meeting; addressing the existing businesses within the town. By wording and structure of the notice, the Reverend could tell that there was a movement going forward to clean up the town and make it more suitable for raising families and not just for making money off of the miners, lumberjacks and other workers in the area. Turning from the poster he saw the young pregnant woman coming towards them. As she came near he spoke up; which startled her in more ways than one.

"Good evening, Miss. Miguire," he tipped his hat but did not move completely out of the way.

She looked up at the man with confusion and a little fear. "Ah, good evening?"

"My name is Mr. Black. I'm the new minister in town."

"Oh," the wall of her defenses began to rise.

"I was wondering if you would be able to join us for services this Sunday."

"Oh," the offer caught her off guard. Obviously the minister didn't know who she was, or what she did. "I don't think, ah, that might not be the best idea."

"Well, I don't want to be disagreeable, but I think it's a very good idea."

The Reverend's sincere smile made Molly feel more at ease, but it didn't change her mind. "Well thank you for the invitation but I'm afraid if you knew, ah, well you wouldn't be asking."

The Reverend looked her straight in the eyes with a look that was both tender and serious. She looked down from his gaze.

"Miss Miguire, I know all I need to know, and it does not change a thing, nor does it change the offer. It is an offer for another way, another life. You think about it."

"Thank you Mr. Black," she looked up, "I will think about it."

"That is all I ask."

He held out his hand and she took it, at which he placed his left hand gently on top of hers. "May God bless you, Miss Miguire. You're in our prayers."

She tried to thank him again but could not get the words out. She could not remember the last time a man had been nice to her out of kindness and not out of lust. She just nodded.

The next day the Reverend gave Mrs. Talbert and Mrs. Carter money to buy some necessities to take Molly, which they did with grace and dignity. The young woman was touched by the gesture and the tears in her eyes showed it. The preacher asked that he remain anonymous in the whole thing. The two ladies said nothing to Molly, but could not remain silent to their husbands.

4

Two days later, a hard rain began which caused a small stream of water to run down the mine shaft, creating a muddy mess for the men to work in. When the noon break came, they remained in the mines entrance to eat, John came and sat down next to the preacher.

"I hear you helped out that girl in town."

"Seemed like the right thing to do."

After a short pause John asked, "Do you really believe what that book says?"

The Preacher let the question hang for a moment. "Yes, I do."

Nothing more was said.

****

The lumber camp was wet and sullen as the sun set behind the wooded mountains to the west. The wood-stove burned hot within the large walled tent where the men sat warming themselves. Murphy McAlister bullied his way into the tent with two other men and crowded up next to the heat, rubbing his hands for warmth.

One of the men he shoved aside spoke up. "Oh, excuse me for standing here, maybe we should all step aside so you have plenty of room. Would you like a cup of coffee while your being an idiot?"

Murphy was grinning at the comments right up until the man called him an idiot. "You best watch 'yer self Fletcher.

That mouth might just get you into trouble."

"Don't worry Fletch," a man off to the side spoke up. "You just call on the name of God and he won't touch 'ya."

Murphy clinched his teeth, and the veins in his neck stuck out as his eyes cut over to the man. But before he could reply another added, "Maybe if ol' Henry were a praying man he wouldn't a' got the stuffin' kicked out of him."

"Could be," another offered, "he was praying when that preacher stepped up to save him."

Fletch grinned, "Never thought I'd see you back down from anything Murph', much less a preacher man."

"Watch it Fletcher," Murphy growled.

"Oh," Fletch raised his hands, "I wouldn't hit a man of the cloth either."

The man off to the side said, "Maybe it weren't the cloth that stopped him. That preacher didn't look like he was gonna' roll over, and from what I hear, he's tough as nails. He wasn't backing down either; Murph' saw that. Didn't 'ya? And I'm not so sure he couldn't take you. You used to be the bull of the woods, but could be you've been shoved off the trail."

Murphy stared at the iron stove in front of him, hating every word spoken and resenting the men that spoke them, but his anger became even more focused on the preacher. He had been humiliated in front of the town, and more than that, in front of the men he worked with. He was backed into a corner with no way out. He turned and left without another word but could still hear a few of the men laughing at him as he walked away in the rain. The two men that had come into the tent with him followed close behind.

****

Sunday morning was clear, bright and fresh with the smell that a good rain always leaves behind. When the Reverend opened the door to go out and bring in some wood he kicked something on the step. It was an old used flour sack. When he brought it inside, he found that it contained a new pair of boots. Sitting down in the chair next to the fire, he held them in his hands and wondered who had left them there, this is where his son found him when he woke.

"Where did those come from?" Mathew asked in surprise.

The Reverend turned them over and looked at the solid new soles. "I don't know, they were on the step in that sack."

Mathew sat down in his chair across from his dad with a bewildered look on his face. He wasn't sure how he was supposed to feel. On one hand he was glad his dad had new boots, yet on the other hand he was disappointed because he had wanted to be the one to buy them.

"Do you know anything about this?" the Reverend asked.

Mathew shook his head, "No, I don't." When he looked up he noticed a tear rolling down his dad's cheek and he realized that God had answered his prayer, just not in the way he had wanted. "I'm glad you got 'em, you needed a pair real bad."

The Reverend simply nodded.

Standing in front of the twenty-two people that had gathered for Sunday service, the Reverend was humbled by the gesture that someone in his congregation had done. He opened his worn out Bible to Mathew 6:25 and began reading.

"Therefore I say unto you, take no thought for your life, what ye shall eat or what ye shall drink; nor yet for your body, what ye shall put on. Is not the life more than meat and the body more than raiment?"

He paused and then continued, "Today I stand before you in a new pair of boots and I do not know from where they have come. I was in great need and my need has been met and I do not know whom to thank. I am humbled and I thank the person or persons, that has done this thing for me and I thank the Lord; for his mercies never fail.

From a dry path through the sea to manna in the desert, from prophets to kings, from giving a man extraordinary strength, to giving a man extraordinary wisdom; God has provided. He provided for the children of Israel and He provided for King David. He provided for Daniel, Shadrach, Meshach and to Abednego. He provided the wine for the wedding and the food for the five thousand. He provided sight for the blind and healing for the lame. He provided for Paul and Silas. He provided from the law to grace and from death to life. He provided the Lamb that takes away the sin of the world. He has provided the faith for you to believe and He has provided an eternity with Him for all that do believe in the name of Jesus Christ, His only begotten Son.

The Lord has provided these boots for me through his servant. But they too will wear out just as this body of mine will wear out. But the Spirit of the living God, that lives within me, is the assurance of eternity in the presence of God. Where rust cannot decay, where thieves cannot break in and steal, where the Lamb is the light. The Lord Himself, shall wipe away all tears, where there is no more death, nor sorrow, nor crying, nor pain because the former things have passed away and all things are made new..."

John stood in the shadows at the edge of the meadow and listened to the man that he thought of as, the only selfless man he had ever met.

****

The song of a grateful man interrupted the Monday morning silence. The Reverend sang out his praise as he walked to the mine with hope in his heart and a skip in his step.

Would you be free from the burden of sin? There's power in the blood, power in the blood; Would you o'er evil a victory win? There's wonderful power in the blood.

The days and weeks went by with the everyday things of life, being interrupted by the unexpected things that accompany people that are in tune with the Lord's will. The greed and debauchery that are found in every mining town were offset by the grace and giving of the believers within the very same town. Rumors brought worries of the possibility of a failing mine, but the faith of the believers was stronger than ever; in spite of it. Day after day, the men went to work in the mine. Day after day, they came home tired and weary.

But the following Sunday brought with it a good many things, that shook a good many people up. But as the Reverend always said, 'all things work together for good to them that love God.' But this was a hard day to see the good, not that it didn't start out good, because it did. The Reverend was as pleased as ever, to look out across the faces of some thirty people. Among them was young Molly Miguire, who had come to church with the Talbert's. And if that wasn't enough, Jackson Carter had come for the first time with his wife and children. He didn't look all that happy about being there, but he was there and he would hear the Word of God. That was all the Reverend longed for, that people would hear the Word; after that, it was up to them. A good number of colored folk had shown up also, they sat with Mr. James along the back wall.

John stood off at the edge of the woods, as always, but this time he had found a place where he could see the Preacher through one of the windows. And so it was, that John was the first to see the four lumberjacks coming down the road to the church. They didn't look like the church going kind, but John had found out by now that people weren't always what they seemed.

The Reverend had already begun his sermon on salvation and grace; when Murphy kicked open the door with a crash. The congregation jumped with a start and a gasp as the men stepped into the church. It was obvious that they weren't there to listen to the gospel. A couple of the men in the church stood up ready to fight but the preacher held out his hands.

"It's all right, it's all right. Have a seat men, thank you, have a seat." The Reverend Black spoke with a calm peaceful smile. "I think they're here to see me, if I'm not mistaken."

"You're damn right about that preacher!" Murphy yelled and then took a couple steps towards him.

"Maybe we should talk in private sir," the Reverend offered, knowing that the man was going to do his best to offend and frighten everyone he could.

"What I have to say can go for the whole lot of you." He cast a hateful glare around the room. "You bunch of weak-kneed, soft-soaped, bible thumpers can all go to hell."

"So you believe in hell," the Reverend said with a smile. "Then you must believe in Heaven too."

The man turned back and stared at the preacher with nothing but pure hate. "I don't believe in anything."

"Now that's hard for me to believe. For a man to be as fired up as you, I would have guessed that man, to have an opinion that was contrary to mine at the very least."

"I do have an opinion about you preacher and I ain't afraid to say it either."

"Well, if you have an opinion then you must believe in it, if you're willing to step into the Lord's house and express it. Wouldn't you say?" The Reverend took a couple steps forward with his Bible under his arm. "How about you and I sit down and talk about it."

"How about you pack up your stuff and leave; take your self-righteous ways and get the hell out of this place. We don't need no hypocrite preacher telling others how they should be living or they'll go to hell for not listening."

The Reverend's face became stern and solid. "I won't be going anywhere, friend."

Murphy walked straight up to him and stood eye to eye. Neither man blinked or moved for what seemed like a very long time. Then he took a step back and the people almost relaxed, but then quick as a thought, the man hit the Reverend right square in the face; snapping his back. The Reverend slowly turned back to the man and looked him straight in the eye once more.

Half dozen men stood up with fire in their eyes, ready for the Reverend to give the word to throw the troublemakers out. But the Reverend gave no such sign; he stood like a rock, unflinching and unmoved. The eyes of the men in the church were begging him to call down the thunder, but he didn't. Murphy was standing ready, but when he saw that the man wasn't going to retaliate, he smirked.

"You dumb son-of-a—" Before he finished the curse he hauled off and hit the Reverend again with everything he had. The Reverend's head snapped back again and this time he took a half-step back to catch himself. Then; just like a timber that was being set in place, he rocked back forward and stood. A trickle of blood ran down his cheek from the first hit and a cut on his lip was already starting to bleed from the second.

Murphy glared at the preacher, wanting nothing more than for the man to hit him back, to defend himself and hit him. But he didn't, he just stood there and took two of the best he had to throw. He'd knocked men out with hits like that, and here stood this man in front of him unmoved.

The men in the church were moving now; they were not going to allow this to go on. The other men with Murphy turned to face them and tensions were at the point of snapping. Then the Reverend spoke up in a strong, calm voice.

"You walk a long and lonesome valley, my friend, and

you walk it all alone. Believing in nothing and yet hating everything. Your life has no meaning, no joy and no peace; and you despise everyone that does. You suffer, so you bring suffering to others, but in the end your hatred will destroy only you. I will pray for you, but I will not fear you. I will forgive you, but I will not leave."

The Reverend stood taller than any man had ever stood in front of the lumberjack. He had no answer, no response to the words that had just cut him down. He looked deep into the eyes of the Preacher and saw no fear and no hatred. He turned and walked out of the church, past the men that had come with him and past John, who stood just outside the doorway. He walked away and did not look back.

After they had left, the Reverend went back to the front and opened his Bible; slowly turning the pages. The crinkled fragile sound of the thin paper being turned could be heard by all. The men were still standing, John was just outside the door looking in and all eyes were on the man in front of them, who again read from the Bible.

"Be strong and courageous. Do not be terrified; do not be discouraged, for the LORD your God will be with you wherever you go."

He closed the Bible and stood silent for a moment. He looked up at the people starring at him and said. "We should rejoice for our salvation and we should weep for the lost. They are blinded and bound by their sins and the sins of this world. We should pray for God's guidance in our lives and for salvation in theirs. Let us pray…"

****

On Monday morning, the Reverend awoke within a great depression. Doubt clouded his mind, and the tentacles of fear fought to entangle him. He prayed fervently and strained to read the scripture. And even though he knew that the forces of the evil one, come strongly and forcefully against those that have received a great victory, the depression still came down upon him.

Mathew saw it on his dad's face, "You all right?"

His dad nodded, "I'll be all right."

"What's wrong?"

The Reverend sighed. "It's not uncommon for people that present the Word of God to be attacked with doubt and fear, soon after they have delivered the message."

"Why do you have doubts?" Mathew couldn't understand after what he had seen yesterday.

"I'm not sure that I did the right thing yesterday. I don't know that anyone will come back after what happened. Maybe I should have handled it differently. I don't know?"

The boy closed his eyes and bowed his head in silent prayer for his dad. When the man looked up and saw what his son was doing, his eyes filled with tears; he also closed his eyes and prayed.

The week went by with much talk about what had happened at the Sunday service. Then late Friday night, the Reverend and Mathew were surprised by a knock at the door. Mathew jumped up to see who it was and when he opened the door, he looked up at the man that filled it. For a moment Mathew just stared, but then he backed up and looked over at his father and then back at John.

"John!" the Reverend smiled and got up quickly. "Come in, come in." Right away he could see a difference in the man's face. "Would you like a cup of coffee?"

John nodded, "Yes, thank you."

He had never heard John say thank you to anybody for anything. "It's not all that good but it is hot."

Mathew had already fetched a cup and was headed for the fire for the coffee. But his attention however, was more on the giant that had just walked into the cabin then it was on the hot handle of the coffee pot.

"Ow!" He jerked his hand back from the hot metal. He glanced over at the two men hoping they hadn't seen, but to his embarrassment, they had. His dad simply smiled. Mathew picked up the leather potholder and poured the coffee.

"Have a seat," the Reverend offered. "This is a welcome surprise. What brings you out so late, my friend?"

"I need to talk," the man said with his eyes on the rough cut, wooden plank floor.

"I'm here to listen," the Reverend replied. He thought about sending Mathew away, but John had not given any indication that he wanted the boy gone, something told him that maybe the boy should hear this.

"I've done some bad things in my life," John said with his head down. "Real bad things." His big hands engulfed the coffee cup as he turned it around and around nervously. "I, ah, I'm not proud of much of anything I done in my whole life, Preacher." He looked up for just a second and then back down. "I only knew one good person in my whole life and that was my Grandma. Ma' died when I was too young to know and Pa' left when I was 'bout ten, so I lived with Grandma and Granddad. Granddad was real mean. He ah, well, he done this to me."

John set the cup on the table and then stood up and took off his shirt. At first the Reverend saw nothing but a mountain of muscles until the man turned around and revealed a back covered with scars.

"Good Lord," he whispered.

Mathew's mouth dropped open; he couldn't believe what he saw.

John pulled the shirt back on and sat down again. "Granddad used to be a bosun on the high seas, and that's the way he figured punishment should be handed out, by the cat's tail. I run off when I was still fairly young and I done some bad things, things that I don't even like to think about. I have been angry my whole life, Preacher. Just, ah, just like Murphy, I ain't no different than him. I ain't never known one minute of peace in my life and I made people suffer 'cause I was suffering, and it's killing me. Slowly but surely it's killing me from the inside out. It's tearing away at me all the time." Tears began to stream down his face. "I don't know what to do."

The Reverend put a firm hand on John's shoulder, "We've all done wrong, and the Bible doesn't make one wrong less than another. It says that sin is sin. It says, that if we know what we should do and don't do it, we've sinned. And it says, that if we break the least of the Laws, we have broken them all. We've all fallen short of God's glory and no one is righteous; no one is good, no one."

John looked up in confusion. "Then how—then there's no hope…"

The Reverend smiled. "But there is hope. God sent his Son Jesus, to be what we could not be; and what we cannot be, is sinless. He lived a sinless life in our place and He became sin for our sake. He took all the wrong things that we have done, He took them upon His shoulders and he died for them. He died for our sins; in our place."

John was still confused. "So where is the hope in that?"

"You're right my friend," the Reverend agreed. "There is no hope in a man that dies. But this man Jesus overcame death. He died for our sins, but death could not hold Him, the grave could not keep Him, and He arose from the dead to live forever. He is the hope of the world; He is our hope, our only hope. And He stands at the door of your heart and knocks. He wants to come and make his home within you, to take you from death to life, from sorrow to joy and from turmoil to peace; and all you have to do is invite Him into your heart."

The big man began sobbing as the tears started running down his face. He nodded and sniffled out the words. "Yes, I want to do that."

Mathew watched this giant of a man cry like a baby in his dad's arms as he accepted Jesus as his Savior. He watched him weep with regret and then weep with joy as he poured out his heart. They would talk and then they would pray; they would talk some more and then his dad would pray some more, and every time they prayed another burden would be lifted from the big man's shoulders. He had a million questions to ask, and he had one of the biggest smiles Mathew had ever seen. His dad said it was because it had been saved up for this very day.

They talked and prayed and drank coffee until early morning, at which point the Reverend made breakfast and then they headed off to the mine. John insisted on learning one of the songs that he had heard at the church, so the Reverend taught him one, and by the time they reached the mine you could hear John's deep booming voice ringing out across the land.

I'm rejoicing night and day,
As I walk the narrow way,
For the hand of God in all my life I see;

And the reason of my bliss,
Yes, the secret all is this:
That the Comforter abides with me.

He abides, He abides;
Hallelujah, He abides with me!

I'm rejoicing night and day,
As I walk the narrow way,
For the Comforter abides with me,

"GOOD MORNING, CLANCY!" John greeted Callaghan on the road up to the mine.

"Ah, good morning to ya', John," the Irishman answered in bewilderment.

"And a bright fine morning it 'tis too," John added with a laugh, mimicking the Irishman's usual morning greeting.

"Yes it 'tis," Callaghan was half afraid the man had lost his mind. He gave the Reverend a look that begged the question, 'what's going on?'

The Reverend grinned from ear to ear. "Mr. Callaghan," he announced, "Our friend John has joined the flock. He is a child of God and his name is written in the Lamb's book of life."

"Well, I'll be damn," Callaghan replied with surprise. "I never saw it coming, no sir. The Lord's wonders never cease."

"Amen!" John proclaimed out loud and then started singing again.

"He abides, He abides
Hallelujah, He abides with me!

By the time they reached the mine, the three men had a good and loud, albeit rough, harmony going which drew the attention of everyone; and even more so when they saw that one of the men was John. The miners gawked in disbelief as the happy men passed by. Some said they must be drunk, while others wagered they had lost their minds.

Chris stepped forward and spoke up. "Nope, Callaghan say's that Big John done got saved."

"Ain't no way!" one miner blurted out.

"You saying John went and got religion?" another questioned.

"Some call it religion," Chris replied. "But if you ever heard that preacher preach, then you'd know John had himself a come-to-meeting with the Almighty. He's been washed in the blood, yes sir, he surely has."

"Ain't no way," the one miner repeated, still in disbelief. "There ain't no way God could look past a man like that."

Chris gave the man a half serious look and said. "You better hope that he can friend; because if He can't look past him… then He can't look past any of us."

It was a day in the mine like none other they had seen, or heard. John sang out the only gospel song he knew, until the men made the Reverend teach him another one, and then he sang it too. He greeted everyone with a smile and shook the hands of men that he hadn't ever spoken to. When the noon break came around, John was sitting right in the middle of everyone.

"You know," Chris started in, "Speaking of heaven (which nobody was), did I ever tell you about the time when I was a kid, just knee high to a grasshopper—well, back then my Mama took me to church every Sunday. Well, I remember this one time the preacher was a going at it like thunder. He was preaching hell fire and brimstone, and then he starts to pointing at people and asking them right then and there, 'Do you want to go to heaven?' at which the first man he pointed at said 'yes.' And then he points to a woman and says, 'Do you want to go to heaven?' to which she replied, 'yes!' And then he looks right at me with those intense firebrand eyes and says, 'Do you want to go to heaven?' Well I snapped back quickly, 'No, no I don't!' That preacher reared back in astonishment and then leaned back towards me again and said, 'Do you mean to tell me that you don't want to go to heaven when you die?' 'Oh,' I said, 'When I die yes. I thought you were getting a group together to go right now.'"

The men grinned and laughed and so did John.

5

Every evening after work John would go to the Reverend's little cabin and have him read the scriptures to him and explain them. The man could simply not get enough; as though a whole new world had been opened up to him. He took everything he heard for what it said, literally.

"They really did that?" John questioned when the Reverend read about the early Christians sharing everything and giving unselfishly to others.

"Yes," he answered. "God has given freely to His own so that they will be able to give, and in this way they are able to represent the love of Christ to all. You see, once we have received the free gift of salvation—that is, once we are born again and become a child of God—we become ambassadors, ah, representatives, for Him. So what we do and how we act is not for our salvation, but because of our salvation. It is the evidence of our faith."

The big man's wrinkled forehead was evidence that he was processing the words and thinking them through. "I think I understand," he nodded. "But what if I mess up? I mean what if I sin again?"

"God is faithful to forgive," the Reverend explained. "Perfection will come when we get to heaven. So when we sin, we should go to God and ask forgiveness and He is faithful to forgive us and set us on the right path. We try so hard to be good, and yet we fail, but that is the very reason God sent His Son. You see, we are not good enough, but Christ was, and is. He lived the perfect life and died in our place, for our sins, to provide a way for us to be saved.

And on and on it went, question after question, scripture after scripture, they read, prayed and talked and then they did it all over again. Mathew watched with renewed interest in the Bible because of the change he was witnessing right before his eyes. This giant of a man who was known for putting fear into men and incapable of compassion, was becoming as gentle as a lamb.

When Saturday came around, all but the blasting crew had the day off, and you could hear the low rumble of distant thunder coming from the mountain all day. Early in the morning, John was at the preacher's door. He was on his way to town to do what the Bible said he was supposed to do. The Reverend thought for a moment that he would go, but he was prompted to do something else.

"I have some things that I need to catch up on around here, but maybe Mathew would like to go along?"

"Would you go with me Mathew?" John asked with hope in his voice. He did not want to do this alone, because he wasn't quite sure how.

"Yeah," he answered, a little nervous, but excited. "I'll go."

"Good," John smiled.

As the two set off for town it struck the Reverend, that John was probably more like a twelve year old now than he had ever been when he was twelve. As they walked along the rutted road to town, John laid a big gentle hand on Mathew's shoulder.

"Your Pa's a good man," he told the boy at his side. "You may not know it, but you're lucky to have a Pa like that. You pay attention to what he says."

"Yes sir," Mathew answered. The boy felt safe with John and at ease enough to ask. "What is it you're going to do in town?"

"Well," John replied, "the Bible says that we should give to those in need. So that's what I'm gonna do. I figure I got more than I need and there's a few folks that don't have enough, so I'm gonna share what I got." He paused. "I, ah, I ain't never done nothing like this ever before. That's why I need your help in doing this."

"I can try," Mathew said. "What do you want to give?"

"I don't know for sure," John confessed. "I've got some money but I don't know if I should give the money or buy something with the money, then give it to them? What do you think?"

"Well…" Mathew thought about it for a moment. "I guess there's nothing wrong with either one. But Dad usually goes ahead and buys the groceries, if he knows that's what they need, so they don't have to. But sometimes he'll give them the money and then sometimes he gives the money to the store and when the people come in, their stuff is already paid for. He does that when he don't want the folks to know who it was that done it."

"Is that better," John asked, "for the folks not to know who done it?"

"I think so," Mathew answered. "Dad says if you give something for the wrong reason, you won't be blessed by it."

"What do you mean?"

"Well," Mathew explained, "if you give something because it makes you look good to others, that isn't right—I mean, you won't get blessed by it. Dad says that your only reward will be the attention you get by the people you wanted to impress. But if you give without letting people know what you're doing, then God will bless you, which is far better than if men bless you. Does that make sense?"

"I think so," John answered. "Fact is, I did just that a while back but I didn't really know what I was doing, if that makes any sense. So maybe we should go on down to the Company store first. Okay?"

"Sounds good to me," Mathew shrugged. "Who is it you're wantin' to help out?"

"Well," John became a little saddened. "That boy that I hit is in bad shape. Too bad off to work and he's got a family and all, so I ah, I thought that maybe I should help 'em out."

"Really? I heard that he was trying to pick a fight that whole night. I heard that he was pushing my Dad around."

"That ain't true," John had a more serious tone to his voice—almost defensive. "I've seen more than my share of tough men, and your Pa is the toughest I ever saw. He could a' turned that boy inside out without even trying. But he didn't. Just like that lumberjack the other day, I'd bet my last dollar that man would of come out on the short end of the stick if your Pa would have let loose on him. But he didn't. I ain't never seen anything like it in all my days, son. I mean, without even throwing one single punch, your Pa sent that man down the road more humbled than if he'd of knocked hell out of 'em," he shook his head as if still in disbelief. "Don't you ever think that 'yer Pa ain't a man fer' not fightin'. I've fought my whole way through life and I ain't never been bested, and I ain't half the man your Pa is." He gave Mathew's shoulder a squeeze. "Yes sir, 'yer a lucky boy. Guess I'm lucky too."

The Company's store clerk stared blankly at John and Mathew. "You want to what?"

"I want to pay off Jackson Carter's account and put money into it for later use," John smiled.

The clerk scratched his head in confusion. "Well, you don't owe anything to the Company, so I guess it's all right. I just don't know, I ah, I haven't ever had to do anything like this before."

"One more thing," John added with a serious look. "You can't tell anyone," he leaned forward a little. "Understand?"

"Yes sir," the clerk replied with all sincerity. "Well I never," he whispered as he turned to get the account book.

"And when you get that down in there, I want to put down some more money for that young lady, Molly Miguire and her baby."

The clerk turned around with a confused look on his face. "You want to give money to that—" He cut short his words when he saw the look John was giving him. "Ahh, all right. It's your money, it doesn't matter to me."

"Remember now," John affirmed. "Not a word to anybody. Right?"

"Right," the clerk shook his head and went about the task at hand.

****

The Reverend walked up the narrow path towards the well built, wooden planked shack that set back off the road in the woods. The plucking sound of a steel guitar could be heard long before he saw the home. Two black men sat out on the porch, one playing and the other singing. He'd been told by one of the congregation that Mr. James could sing and his cousin could play the steel guitar and that they could do it very well.

The two men kept singing and playing, even though they saw the Reverend approaching. He walked up and leaned against the porch post and listened to the rhythmic tune. The music and the words created a sense of peace within him that made the worries, that he didn't even think he had, drift away on an unseen cloud. When the words of the song were finished, Mr. James' cousin kept up the music for at least another two to three minutes, to the enjoyment of the other two men. When the last note drifted off into the treetops there was a moment of silence before Mr. James spoke.

"Reverend, what brings you to our part of the world?"

"You do, Mr. James," he answered, "you and your cousin."

"I ain't ever been called on by a preacher man a'fore," Cousin James replied. "I feel right special."

"What is it you want from us Reverend?" Mr. James asked.

"I want you to sing at tomorrow's service," the Reverend grinned.

"Oh, now Reverend sir," Mr. James responded with wide eyes. "You done some odd things since you been here, but this one beats all I ever heard."

"I don't see the problem Mr. James," he answered. "You can both sing and I have a special song in mind for you."

"If you can't see the problem Reverend, then you can't see at 'all," Cousin James said.

"I'm simply asking you to use the gifts God gave you to bless others. Is that too much to ask?"

Mr. James frowned at the use of scripture to strong arm him. "That ain't fair." Mr. James rubbed his chin in turmoil thought.

"I'll take full responsibility," the Reverend added.

"I've no doubt you would, Mr. Black," Mr. James replied half-serious. "But that won't stop the way folks will likely react to what you want, that will come down on us," he paused and then said, "I'll sing for you, but I'll do it from the back of the church. Cousin James can decide for his self."

"I'll sing with Edward, in the back," Cousin James added.

"Mr. James," the Reverend scolded. "There is neither Jew nor Greek, there is neither bond nor free, there is neither male nor female: for ye are all one in Christ Jesus."

"Yes sir," Mr. James said, "but it also says to give no offense, neither to the Jews nor to the Gentiles, nor to the church, not seeking my own profit but the profit of many that they may be saved."

The Reverend had been bested at his own game and he knew it.

"Reverend sir," Mr. James added. "Is it more important for the people to hear the song or see me sing it?" he paused and then went on. "Maybe someday I'll sing right up front in your church, but that ain't this day. It is what it is and you can't force it to be different."

The Reverend took a deep breath and then sighed. "Very well, I apologize for speaking of things I don't know," he handed a piece of paper to Mr. James. "Here is the song. If you do not wish to sing tomorrow, I will hold no ill thought of it. If you wish to sing, then simply nod to me and I will have you sing at the close of service. And, I will make it so you will not be put on display for my own arrogant pride. Forgive me."

Mr. James smile returned. "Don't you go fretting on this, Reverend. Took God six days to make this here world. Took mankind a many thousand years to make it this bad and you ain't gonna go making it all better in one day. But I do admire your determination to try. Have a seat and let's see what this here song can do. He opened up the paper and began reading the words as the Reverend hummed the tune.

The Sunday morning sun looked down on a little country church that was full of people. Some came to hear the word of God, some came to see the preacher that they had heard so much about. And some came to see if it was true about the man called John. Whatever the reason, they were here and the church was full and the Reverend was pleased.

The Reverend ended his sermon. "Grace is getting what we don't deserve. Mercy is not getting what we do deserve and Judgment is getting exactly what we do deserve. Where do you stand today? On the promises of God and under His all-sufficient Grace, or are you trying to stand on your own? Where do you stand today?" He then looked to the back of the room at Mr. James who nodded gently.

"I want everyone to close their eyes and listen to the words of the song you are about to hear. Please, close your eyes, thank you. Now listen to the words."

Mr. James began singing in perfect harmony with his cousin's music.

> "I heard an old, old story,
> How a Savior came from glory.
> How He gave His life on Calvary,
> To save a wretch like me.

As the song went on the tears began to flow and they rolled down the cheeks of many; among them were Molly Miguire and John.

> "O victory in Jesus,
> My savior, forever.
> He sought me and bought me
> With His redeeming blood;
> He loved me ere I knew Him,
> And all my love is due Him,
> He plunged me to victory,
> Beneath the cleansing flood.

On Monday morning Jackson Carter went to town to make arrangements for paying his credit, it was coming due and he was going to try and get an extension. He walked in with the hope that his being able to go back to work would gain some leniency with the Company.

"Hello," he said humbly to the clerk. "My names' Jackson Carter and my credit payment is coming due and I'd like to make arrangement to pay it out on time, if I could, please."

"Yes, Jackson Carter," the name was still fresh in the clerk's mind. "It's been taken care of."

"What do you mean?"

"What I mean is; you don't owe anything, your debt has been paid off," the clerk leaned on the counter. "And what's more, you have credit with Company."

"That can't be?" he was confused. "I owe the Company money. How can I have more credit available? You've made a mistake."

"No sir, I haven't," the clerk replied. "Someone came in and paid off your account and added to your credit."

"Who would do that?"

"Can't say," the clerk's mind flashed back to the huge figure that had loomed over the counter and told him not to tell.

"What do you mean you can't say?" Jackson was getting angry. "That's my account and I want to know!"

"Why don't you just be glad for it son," the clerk grinned. "It isn't very often a man gets a gift like that."

"I don't need nobody's charity!"

"Oh really?" the clerk raised an eyebrow. "Isn't that what you were wanting from the Company when you walked in here? Weren't you going to try and make a deal with me to pay this off in time? Well, isn't that what you were going to do?"

"That's my business, not some strangers," he said through clenched teeth.

"Well maybe that's true," the clerk gave the man a disgusted look. "But it is my business; and your credit stays paid off. Now whether you use it or not, is up to you. But in your condition, you're a fool if you don't."

Jackson Carter set his teeth as his hands gripped the edge of the counter. The clerk shook his head at the man's stubbornness, shrugged his shoulders and said, "Do what you feel's best." He walked away from the counter; leaving the angry man to himself.

That very same day found Molly Miguire in her room staring out the window and wondering how she was going to feed herself that day, and the day after…and the day after that. The Talberts had been such a help to her, but they could not afford to supply all her needs. She didn't know what to do. The baby within her kicked, and she wished she could be happier about it.

The knock at the door brought her out of her trance; she struggled to get up and drag herself to the door. Upon opening it; see was surprised to see the twelve year old boy standing there.

"Miss Miguire?"

"Yes?" she replied softly.

"This is for you ma'am." He held out a folded piece of paper.

"Thank you," she took the paper. "Who's it from?"

"The Company clerk, ma'am," the boy answered.

"Thank you," she said.

"Yes ma'am," he tipped his cap and left.

Molly went back over to her chair at the window and eased herself down into it as she unfolded the paper.

Dear Miss Miguire,

Your account at the Company store has been settled and paid in full. You also have credit with the store; available to you at your convenience. See Company Clerk for amount.

Gregory Stubben

Company Clerk

Molly pressed the paper to her chest and closed her eyes; it was an answer to her prayers. She smiled at the thought of God answering her prayer while she sat in this place. Maybe God could do something about her circumstances.

****

Every Sunday, John was the first one to church and the last one to leave. As hard and solemn as he had been before, he was that much more enthusiastic and outspoken in his faith. He believed what the Bible said, every word that he could understand, but most of all he believed that God loved him and that Jesus died for him and that he was a changed man because of it.

Then one ordinary day as the men worked down in the mine something happened—something that changed everything, forever. They had been doing a lot more blasting than usual, trying to uncover a profitable vein of coal, but they weren't having much luck. The men picked apart every inch they could and hoped that things would take a turn for the better. They didn't.

On this particular day there were twenty-one men down in the mine when a rumble deep in the earth brought everyone to a standstill. They froze with fear at the sound.

"Oh, good God Almighty save us," one miner breathed out.

"Get out! Everyone! Now!" Callaghan shouted.

"Let's go!" Chris yelled as they all started up out of the mine.

Another rumble sent tremors through the dark damp mine and through the men. Every man down there would be a liar if they denied thinking that this cold black hole might be their grave. In their minds, the walls were closing in on them with every rumble; they could see the end coming in a pitch-black coffin filled with miners. They scrambled and scratched their way towards the opening as fast as they could, their hearts pounded within their chest as if they would explode. Some cried out in desperation and others were too scared to speak, and still others prayed.

"God no, please God no!"

"I don't want 'a die down here!"

"Hurry up, come on! Get out 'a the way!"

"Lord protect us."

"Keep going!"

"She's cavin' in boys."

Up ahead of the men, a huge rock crashed to the mineshaft floor sending up dirt and dust to fill the air. They worked their way past the rock; coughing and choking on the thick heavy dust. They were getting close. These men had walked this mine too many times not to know exactly where they were, and how far it was to get out. They could hear the mine caving in behind them and just as soon as the rumble died down, the men in the lead heard the unmistakable sound of a timber cracking.

Rocks tumbled down as the huge timber started to split and sag. They stopped and watched as it creaked its way down towards the floor of the mine. The options of what to do raced through their minds. The beam was going to give way at any moment and anybody under it would be killed for sure. If they stayed where they were, the mine could cave in on them where they stood.

But before anyone could say anything, the huge shadow of a man walked past them through the black dust; without hesitation he stooped down under the sagging timber, placing the beam across his wide shoulders he whispered, "The Lord is my strength," they watched in fear and amazement as this giant of a man let out with a groan, that sounded more like the rolling of far away thunder. With all of the strength within his body and soul, John pushed against the timber. The men held their breath and hoped beyond hope that he could do this. The timber creaked again, but this time it was going up.

"There's a light!" a miner yelled. "I see a light let's go!"

"Move it!" Chris yelled. "Hurry! Go! Go! Go!"

Twenty men ran past the human oak that held up the beam. The men in the lead were shouting out to the men outside to get jacks and timbers. The last one past John was the Reverend. He stopped on the other side and yelled to him.

"Come on John! Come on!"

"Go!" John yelled. "It's gonna' all come down, get out. Go!"

John's legs began to quiver under the weight. He looked up at the Reverend who was slowly backing up, as if two opposing forces were pulling at him. The big man's eyes met his, and for a split second he saw John smile. It was a smile of peace. A smile that said, 'it's okay'. A smile that said, 'I'm going home.'

A rock came down between them and the dirt filled the shaft as the man was hidden from his sight. He turned and ran as hard as he could towards the entrance of the mine as he shouted, "Jacks! Bring the jacks! Hurry!"

Just as he was about to reach the entrance, a loud thunder came from the dark cavern behind him. It rolled and grumbled and shook the ground, sending bellows of dirt and dust up the shaft past him and out of the mouth and into the air. Everyone knew that it was done. As the Reverend walked out of the cloud of dirt boiling from the mouth of the mine, the rumbling sound of a complete cave in rolled up behind him. He turned and looked back down into the cave, he could still see him in his mind, standing there smiling, knowing what was about to happen.

****

Everyone was there. The whole town came out on that bright sunny day when they set the headstone at the entrance of the mine. The Company said that the mine wasn't worth opening up to work again, but they would dig it out if that's what would be best. The miners agreed that there was no need, and that the mine was the only grave big enough for John anyhow. The Reverend said it didn't matter; John wasn't down there any ways; so they could do as they pleased. He stood up and spoke to all that had gathered.

"I did not know John for very long," he paused. "But in that short time I came to know him very well. Not the man of anger and fear, but the man of love and gentleness, the man of compassion and grace.

"Let me tell you how much this man had changed. The day that my son and I arrived in this town, we spent the early morning with a wagon stuck in the mud. While we were trying to free the wagon, a man walked by us and never lifted a finger to help. He didn't so much as cast a glance in our direction and he didn't tell anyone that we needed help either. That was the same man—," the Reverends voice cracked. "That was the same man that gave his life for twenty other men, and he did it with a glad heart. I know because I saw him at the end, and he smiled. He smiled as a man that was going home.

"If you ask how it's possible for a man to change from being completely selfish to completely selfless, it was by the Love and Grace of God. John had become a new creation. His old self was falling away and his new self was growing every day.

"Greater love hath no man than this, that he lay down his life for his friends. And that is what John did for us, because that is what Jesus did for him. If I have ever met a man that knew the Grace of God, it was my friend John.

"I mourn for my loss, and yet I rejoice for my friend. He has gone home to be with the Lord in the place that was prepared for him.

"For all of John's life, he was known for being a big man and he was the biggest man that I have ever met. But I hope that from this day on you will remember John as I do; for I will always remember him as a big man, with an even bigger heart."

He looked over at Mr. James who acknowledged the look with a nod. Cousin James pulled his guitar from behind his back and began playing 'Amazing Grace.' After he had played through the chorus once, Mr. James began singing.

A marble headstone was placed at the entrance of the mine, it read simply,

HERE LIES JOHN
HE WAS A BIG MAN
****

A few days later a message was sent to the Reverend that he was needed at the Company Storr, to take care of some unfinished business. He and Mathew made the long quiet walk together.

"I was told that there was some unfinished business for me?"

"Not your business necessarily," the clerk replied. "But I didn't know what else to do with it." He brought out the account book and opened it up on the counter.

"John had money coming to him and since there's no next of kin; that we know of, you're the closest that we're going to find." He looked at the Preacher over his thin rimed round glasses. "It's a decent amount, we trust you will know what to do with it."

The Reverend held up his hands as if to push the offer away. "Surely the Company has had to deal with these things before, I don't know if this is the best thing to do."

The clerk went on as if he hadn't heard a word. "And there is the matter of Jackson Carter also."

"What have I got to do with his account?"

"Your friend John paid off the Carter's account in full and also added funds to the account; so that he could feed his family I suppose," the clerk pointed to the amount that had been deposited. "It's all there. Carter hasn't used one penny of it and says he won't use it either. I have contacted the young man numerous times to use the funds or he'll lose them. He has emphatically rejected all offers; therefore I am also rolling these funds back into John's account."

"I don't think this is—"

"Miss Miguire, on the other hand," the clerk continued; interrupting the Reverend, "was more than thankful and actually cried. She begged to know who the giver was so that she could thank them. But I had promised not to tell," the clerk looked up. "I haven't said a word to anyone, only you and the boy know anything about all this."

The Reverend looked over at Mathew, "Is this what you and John did that day you came into town?"

Mathew nodded in confirmation, "It's what he wanted to do."

The Reverend rubbed his chin as he thought the situation through. The clerk was leaning forward with both hands on the counter awaiting a reply.

"I can pay it out in cash if you want, or I can roll it all over into your account. Which will it be?"

The Reverend looked up with a slight grin, "Neither."

"Now Preacher," the clerk straightened up.

"For I say unto you," he began, "that unto every one which hath shall be given; and from him that hath not, even that he hath shall be taken away from him."

"What?" the clerk replied with a look of confusion.

"Mr. Carter has rejected the gift of a very generous man

and therefore he shall lose what was offered to him. May God protect his family," the Reverend continued. "But Miss Miguire, on the other hand, has accepted with humility and thanksgiving the very same gift and therefore; she will be given more so that her thanksgiving will continue."

"Right," the clerk stared back blankly. "So…you want me to give the money to Miss Miguire?"

"That is exactly what I want."

"Ah," the clerk scratched his head. "It's a goodly sum of money. John didn't really buy much of anything lately, except for a pair of boots."

"A pair of boots?"

"Yep."

The Reverend looked down at the new boots on his feet and then back up at the clerk.

The clerk asked again. "Are you sure you want this money going to Miss Miguire?"

"Quite sure," the Reverend confirmed.

"Well I never," the clerk sighed. "All right."

"Write out a check, and we'll take it to her right now," the Reverend urged. "You write on the check who it's from also."

"From you?" the clerk questioned.

"No!" the Reverend snapped back. "It's from John and I think it would be all right for her to know that. Right, Mathew?"

"Yes sir," Mathew nodded to the clerk. "I think she should know."

Molly Miguire had her baby two weeks later, she named him John. She also moved out of the boarding house and in with the Talberts for a while. The money she had received not only helped her, but also the Talberts as they waited for the mine to begin work on the new shaft, which it did.

Jackson Carter became a mean, embittered man while his wife remained faithful in prayer and service to the Lord and her children.

Chris and Callaghan went back to work for the Company as soon as work on the new shaft began. Mr. James and Cousin James continued splitting and supplying wood for the businesses in town and building houses for the new people that came along.

The Reverend remained in the mining town as the preacher and as a miner until the Lord sent him on to another place, another town, and another adventure. He preached the Word of God wherever he went, he helped the needy, and he resisted the proud, and he never forgot his friend John, I know, because the Reverend Mr. Black was my Dad.

What makes a man the way he is? I'm still not sure. But what changes a man—is his heart.

Acknowledgements

This story was inspired by the song, Big John, written and performed by Jimmy Dean.

Also, by the song, Reverend Mr. Black, written by Ed Wheeler, Mike Stoller, and Jerry Leiber.

CPSIA information can be obtained at www.ICGtesting.com
265431BV00001B/1/P